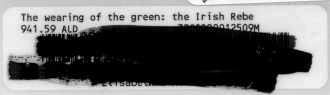

THE WEARING OF THE GREEN
The Irish Rebellion (1916–21)

The Irish Rebellion began with the ill-fated Easter Week Rising of 1916. The Irish rising was brutally crushed; but Irish rebel influences grew in the British Parliament, and the Irish rebels waged undeclared war with Britain at home. An Irish Republic with allegiance to the Crown was declared in 1921, setting the stage for an even more disgraceful and violent conflict—civil war. Finally, in 1948, a bloody chapter in Irish history closed with the creation of the free Republic of Ireland—but the seeds were laid for the violence and bitterness which continue to plague this strife-ridden nation. Maps and photos.

BOOKS BY
CLIFFORD LINDSEY ALDERMAN

The Wearing of the Green

THE IRISH REBELLION (1916-21)

By Clifford Lindsey Alderman

maps & photographs

*O Paddy dear, an' did ye hear the news
that's goin' round?
The shamrock is by law forbid to grow on
Irish ground!
No more St. Patrick's Day we'll keep, his
colour can't be seen,
For there's a cruel law agin the wearin' o'
the Green!
I met wid Napper Tandy, and he took me
by the hand,
And he said, "How's poor ould Ireland,
and how does she stand?"
She's the most disthressful country that iver
yet was seen,
For they're hangin' men and women there
for wearin' o' the Green!*

JULIAN MESSNER   NEW YORK

Published by Julian Messner
a division of Simon & Schuster, Inc.
1 West 39th Street, New York, N.Y. 10018
All Rights Reserved

Second Printing, 1973

For Jack Meaney, who fought for it.

941.59
A

Library of Congress Cataloging in Publication Data

Alderman, Clifford Lindsey.
  The wearing of the green.

  SUMMARY: Discusses the historical background and events of
the five-year uprising that led to Irish independence after nearly
800 years of British rule.
  Bibliography: p. 184
  1. Ireland—History—1910-1921—Juvenile literature. [1. Ireland—
History—1910-1921] I. Title. II. Title: The Irish Rebellion.
DA962.A67   941.59   72-1832
ISBN 0-671-32552-3
ISBN 0-671-32553-1 (lib. bdg.)

Printed in the United States of America

ACKNOWLEDGMENTS

Grateful acknowledgment is made to the following for the generous assistance given me in many ways in the writing of this book:

Dr. and Mrs. C. S. Andrews, Dundrum, Dublin; Gerry Cosnin, Neenagh, Tipperary; Seamus Kelly of the *Irish Times*, Dublin; Kevin Kilgariff, Tuam, Galway; Mr. and Mrs. H. M. S. Miller, Dublin; Mrs. Nora Connolly O'Brien, Dublin; Ralph A. Sherman, Columbus, Ohio; and the American-Irish Historical Society, New York, N. Y.

CONTENTS

Dublin in 1916

Chapter 1

EIGHT CENTURIES of PERSECUTION and SUFFERING

IN SEVERAL WAYS the day in 1916 when the Irish patriots started their final, successful struggle for freedom from the long, unjust and often cruel rule of England was not unlike the day in 1775 when the American colonies' war for the same thing began. In both cases it was April. Both were rising against the rule of Britain. The leaders of both knew how small was the chance to win a military victory over such great military might. And although the Irish rebels were forced into unconditional surrender during the Easter Week of 1916, while the American patriots won a smashing though minor victory on April 19, 1775, both were just as far from independence at the end of this first fighting. Yet in the end both won.

There were other similarities. The men on the green in Lexington in 1775 were a group of simple farmers, carrying old flintlock muskets. In Dublin on Easter Monday, April 24, 1916, the rebels were largely simple workingmen with old weapons—single-barreled shotguns and ancient German Howth Mausers made for the Franco-Prussian War of 1870. Neither the Irish rebels of 1916 nor the Americans at Lexington in 1775 had artillery.

As with the Americans at Lexington, the number of Irish who turned out was small. In all, they had about 1,200 men. If all the members of the Irish Volunteers and the Irish Citizen Army in Dublin had assembled, there would have been twice as many. If, all over Ireland, these groups had risen in rebellion, there would have been 10,000. And if every man in Ireland who had had at least some military training had responded to the call to arms, the country would have had 100,000 men in rebellion that day.

Ireland's troubles with England began in the year 1171, when King Henry II of England invaded the island to the west. They continued, off and on, for nearly eight centuries.

Ireland was colonized untold ages ago by various peoples, but each in time was driven out by the next. The last were the Celts, or Gaels, who were supposed to have come from Spain. They formed the real beginning of the Irish nation.

The next great invasion was by those fierce sea marauders, the Norsemen, about the year 795. In 1014 the famous Irish chieftain Brian Boru broke the Norse power forever at the battle of Clontarf, though he himself was killed.

For over a century after that the Irish enjoyed peace. They had proved themselves fierce fighters at Clontarf, but at heart they were peace-loving people. And with the coming of St. Patrick, who was not even born in Ireland, as a missionary in 432, bringing the Catholic religion there, Ireland's rise to the greatest center of learning in Europe had begun.

Poets and writers flourished. Britons, Saxons, Welshmen and Bretons from Brittany flocked to Ireland to absorb learning from the great Irish scholars. Irish missionaries spread the Gospel in what are now England, Germany, France, Italy, Belgium and Switzerland. The scholars themselves traveled throughout Europe, teaching grammar, mathematics, astronomy, geography, theology and science.

There were expert Irish workers in gold, silver and other metals. Today exquisite examples of their art are prized by museums everywhere. Scribes did the laborious task of writing books in a script so fine that it resembles printing, with many of the letters illuminated in bright colors. Today thousands of tourists visit Trinity College in Dublin to see the famous Book of Kells, done by Irish monks in the eighth century.

The peaceful Irish countryside was dear to its people, who were mostly farmers. Ireland is well named the Emerald Isle. Its mild climate and frequent rainfall make it green indeed. It is a beautiful land. All over the island are scenic areas with spectacular mountains, lakes, streams and coasts. Unlike its neighbor England, across the Irish Sea, Ireland is sparsely populated. And while its larger cities teem with motor traffic, on its country roads one sees mostly carts, jaunting cars and other vehicles pulled by horses or donkeys. Yet for almost eight centuries this peaceful-looking country was constantly torn by wars, uprisings, persecution, famine and suffering.

When Henry II came to Ireland in 1171, he divided most of the island between himself, his Norman subjects from Wales, who had invaded and settled Ireland a little earlier, and the Irish chieftains who made submission to him, expecting they would go on ruling their clans as before.

These chieftains found out, too late, that they had become mere puppets of the Anglo-Norman conquerors, who were too powerful to be resisted. During the next eighty years, three-quarters of Ireland was under the control of the invaders.

The Anglo-Normans did make improvements in Ireland. A better system of government and justice was introduced. Although the Norse invaders had established coastal towns like Dublin, Wexford, Cork, Waterford and Limerick, there were almost none inland. The new conquerors built them. Since they also were Catholic, they brought in monks of several religious orders new to Ireland and built some fine cathedrals.

But by the year 1300, Norman supremacy was weakening. For one thing, most of the Irish chieftains had never been conquered, and the clans in the wild, mountainous regions were always a threat. But the strongest influence was intermarriage between the Gaelic Irish and the Normans. It made the English government decide that something had to be done before a revolt could end its supremacy over Ireland. An Irish Parliament, controlled by the great landowners loyal to England, had been established. In 1366 it passed the Statutes of Kilkenny, which forbade these intermarriages under severe penalties. But the new laws had little effect; intermarriage went on.

Henry VIII and some of his successors to the English crown were less successful in imposing the Reformation upon devoutly Catholic Ireland than they had been in England. The Reformation in England began when the Pope in Rome refused to annul Henry VIII's marriage to Catherine of Aragon so that he could marry Anne Boleyn. The enraged Henry broke with the Church of Rome and had himself declared the Supreme Head of the Church in England, which gradually became Protestant in form.

In England, practically all Catholic monasteries were destroyed and their wealth and possessions seized. In Ireland the Reformation had little effect except in the larger, English-controlled towns, where religious houses were dissolved.

When Queen Mary I, a staunch Catholic, came to the English throne in 1553, the Church of Rome was restored, but her sister, Elizabeth I, brought back the Protestant Church of England, and began to extend it to Ireland. For a time she was foiled by a great Irish hero, Shane O'Neill. With his army he successfully resisted all attempts to abolish the Catholic Church in his homeland of Northern Ireland.

Elizabeth invited Shane the Proud, as he was called in Ireland, to England, but failed to charm him into yielding. For five years he ruled in Ulster, and it remained Catholic. Shane died at the hands of his own enemies, who slew him at a banquet. Shortly after that a gift was brought into the English Council Chamber of Dublin Castle—Shane the Proud's head. The English Lord Deputy, or governor of Ireland, had it tarred and stuck on a pole at one of the castle gates, and lost no time in writing the good news to Queen Elizabeth.

Then, in 1579, there was a severe rebellion in Munster, the southwest province of Ireland, that was not crushed until 1583. Elizabeth punished the landowners there by taking away 200,000 acres of their property and giving it to loyal English colonists.

From then on Elizabeth seemed to be making progress in her plan to abolish the Catholic religion in Ireland. Strangely, it was Ulster in the north, today a Protestant stronghold, that could not be subdued. In 1595 Hugh O'Neill, the Earl of Tyrone, led the Ulster rebels in a revolt. He fought the English with ambushes and swift raids, and by 1601 he had an army of almost 10,000 men.

The Queen sent Lord Mountjoy to govern Ireland. A

heartless man, he burned crops and houses to make the Ulstermen yield, but they fought on until they were routed at the battle of Kinsale, and Tyrone surrendered. What was called the Nine Years' War was over, and Ireland was conquered.

For nearly forty years the Irish were unable to start another serious revolt. Then, in 1641, they rose again against their masters, gained control of most of Ulster and marched southward. They advanced close to Dublin, and their seizure of Dublin Castle was prevented only because the plan was betrayed to the English. Reinforcements from England then gained an uneasy control that continued until 1649.

When King Charles I was executed in that year, the Puritan Oliver Cromwell seized the rule of England as Protector. He went after the still turbulent Irish with horrifying ferocity. "Cromwell's Curse," as it was called, has never been forgotten in Ireland.

In August, 1649, Cromwell himself led a trained, well-equipped army of 17,000 men to Ireland. They struck first at Drogheda, on the coast north of Dublin. Cromwell reported that about three thousand were killed there, but it would seem that the slaughter of innocent men, women and children as well as the soldiers of Drogheda's garrison was much greater than that.

Cromwell then captured other strongholds in the north and turned south to Wexford, taking several towns on the way. In Wexford the butchery was as savage as at Drogheda. Cromwell then went on to take Cork and other cities.

More than 30,000 Irish soldiers who surrendered and were not massacred were allowed to go into the armies of European countries friendly to England. Many of the few young men left in Ireland, as well as young women, boys and girls, were exiled to America and the West Indies. It has been estimated that between the rebellion of 1641 and Cromwell's ruthless invasion of 1649, Ireland's population was reduced from 1,466,000 to 616,000 people.

Cromwell's revenge knew no bounds. The Catholic landowners and their tenants remaining in Ireland were pushed out of the vast, fertile area east and south of the great River Shannon into the poor country west of it.

The Irish Catholics got back some of their land when Charles I's son, Charles II, regained the English throne, because, although he was a Protestant, he was indebted to many Irishmen who had aided him in exile. They got back more of their rights when Charles II's brother, the Catholic James II, succeeded to the throne. James was soon toppled from it, however, and the Protestants William and Mary came from Holland to rule England.

The Irish Catholics were only too glad to help the deposed James try to get back his crown. But their hopes were shattered when the army he gathered in Ireland was routed by King William's army in the famous battle of the Boyne.

King William offered the Irish what seemed like good terms—religious freedom and the restoration of some of the Irish Catholics' lands. The Irish agreed—and got instead the Penal Laws of the period beginning in 1695 and extending well into the eighteenth century.

The Penal Laws forbade Catholics to vote, hold office, enter military or civil service, practice law or teach school. Only Protestant schools were permitted. A Catholic could not even own a horse if it was worth more than £5. And they were forbidden to marry Protestants. All Catholics who had aided the deposed James II were declared outlaws and their property seized.

Furthermore, to suppress the Catholic religion, one of the Penal Laws banished all members of monasteries, all bishops and most priests from Ireland. Nevertheless, the devout Catholics held secret Masses in secluded spots and private homes.

The result of all this was that thousands of Irish Catholic farmers were poverty-stricken, barely able to feed themselves and their families on the potatoes which fortunately grew extremely well in the Irish climate. Jonathan Swift, the famous poet and author of *Gulliver's Travels,* who was not a Catholic but dean of the Protestant St. Patrick's Cathedral in Dublin, was enraged over the Irish people's sufferings and wrote a number of tracts about the iniquitous Penal Laws. In one he urged that everything coming into Ireland from Britain be burned except its coal. In another sarcastic essay he suggested that the English fatten Irish children and serve them up at dinner.

The Penal Laws failed to suppress the Catholic Church, but they restricted Irish trade and caused such losses to Northern Irish manufacturing that a large emigration of Scotch-Irish to America began. The son of one of these emigrants, Andrew Jackson, became a famous general and then President of the United States. And out of nine signers of the Declaration of Independence who had Irish blood, four had been born in Ireland.

The common people of Ireland sympathized strongly with the American colonies in their struggle for freedom. And Britain's participation in the American Revolution left few British troops in Ireland. Volunteer corps of Irishmen were formed all over the island to seize this chance for their own freedom. By 1780 there were 30,000 volunteers enrolled to fight if necessary. Britain became so alarmed that the Penal Laws were relaxed.

The success of the French common people in the French Revolution, beginning in 1789, also heartened the Irish. A young Protestant lawyer, Wolfe Tone, formed the Society of United Irishmen in 1791. It forced the British government to grant the oppressed people still more relief. Then, during her war with Britain in 1793, the French commissioned Tone a general. He sailed to invade Ireland in 1796 with a French fleet and 15,000 soldiers, but storms drove the expedition back.

Tone tried again in 1798. With another French force he landed in Ireland, where his United Irishmen joined him. Britain sent a powerful force to Ireland under command of Lord Cornwallis, the same general who had made the final surrender in the American Revolution at Yorktown. The British routed Tone's force, captured him and sentenced him to hang like a common criminal, but Tone cheated them of humiliating him by committing suicide in his cell.

Next it was Robert Emmett who tried, bravely but foolishly, for Irish freedom in 1803. Emmett had expected two thousand men to join him from Dublin and the surrounding countryside. Only about eighty showed up, and the planned attack on Dublin Castle failed miserably. Emmett was executed, but at his trial he spoke words that inspired Irishmen in the years of struggle ahead: "When my country takes her place among the nations of the earth, then, and not till then, let my epitaph be written."

A mighty man, Daniel O'Connell, who could sway people to his way of thinking with his oratory, took his seat in the British Parliament in 1829. He forced the British to grant almost full recognition of Catholic rights, but his final effort to achieve the separation of Ireland from Britain failed. Nevertheless, he is one of Ireland's great heroes. Today,

O'Connell Street in Dublin is dominated by his huge statue in its center.

Between 1845 and 1847 the Great Famine threatened to wipe out the Irish people and set back for years their struggle for freedom. The small Irish farmers lived almost entirely on potatoes. In 1845 a blight ruined the crop over half of Ireland. In 1846 the entire crop was destroyed by it. By the spring of 1847 conditions in the country were so frightful as to be indescribable.

All over the country people starved to death. To make matters worse, an epidemic of disease swept the island. So many people died that there were no coffins to bury them in; indeed, in some mountain sections the dead were simply left on the ground, unburied. In some small villages everyone perished. Farmers did grow wheat and oats, but had to sell them to pay the rent or their landlords would evict them. Meanwhile, the big landowners continued to export grain, beef, pork and lamb at a good profit.

Britain's feeble efforts to provide food to ease the Irish people's suffering were little short of disgraceful. Although the government did buy about £100,000 worth of American Indian corn and cornmeal, set up soup kitchens in the large towns and established work projects that employed about 140,000 people, the meat and grain exports went right on, and so did evictions by the landlords of people who could not pay their rent. The landowners then tore down the miserable hovels their tenants had lived in.

Those who could manage it got out, usually sailing to Liverpool in England. By June, 1847, it was estimated that 300,000 destitute people had gone there, and in that year 100,000 sailed for the United States. Smaller ships sailed from Irish ports direct to America, so crammed with people who were little more than living skeletons that they were known as "coffin ships." Many of these wretched passengers died during the voyage.

During the Great Famine over 700,000 people starved or died of fever, and more than 800,000 left the country. Between 1845 and 1861 Ireland lost nearly two million of her population, and because evictions continued, another million left in the next ten years. In America the Irish immigrants persevered, worked hard and became an important force in American life, rising to wealth and high office, even the Presidency.

The Great Famine left Ireland exhausted. Not until 1867 were thousands who had enrolled in the Irish Republican Brotherhood or Fenian movement able to revolt. They failed miserably, but the movement lived on to take an important part in the revolt of 1916. And in 1875 a young Protestant, Charles Stewart Parnell, led a strong effort as a member of Parliament in behalf of the poor tenant farmers still being evicted by the harsh and powerful landlords. He too failed, but he had done much to prepare the Irish for later struggles to obtain their rights.

A quarter of a century later, in 1905, a new champion of Irish liberty, Arthur Griffith, founded Sinn Fein (a Gaelic name, pronounced "Shin Fane," meaning "We Ourselves"). Both Sinn Fein and the Irish Republican Brotherhood grew in strength during the early years of the twentieth century. And in the mountains around Dublin, Countess Markievicz was taking a group of boys on camping trips and drilling and marching them. Before 1916 they would be in the Irish Volunteers.

By 1912 the Irish Party in the House of Commons had become so strong that the British decided to give Ireland Home

Rule. This simply meant that Ireland would have a parliament to govern itself—with the British Parliament able to kill any law the Irish Parliament passed. The new leaders of Ireland's demand for freedom, like Arthur Griffith, Padraic Pearse, James Connolly and Eamon de Valera, wanted none of it.

That a great many of the Irish people had no hatred for Britain and felt a close bond with her was proved when thousands of Irishmen flocked to the colors when the war began in 1914, and fought side by side with Englishmen and Scots in France.

But the men who were dedicated to freedom for Ireland saw that, with Britain engaged in a desperate struggle with Germany and Austria in which her existence was at stake, this was the very time for a revolt. No one knew this better than such patriot leaders as Griffith, Pearse, Connolly and de Valera. The Irish Volunteers of Sinn Fein and the Irish Republican Brotherhood, as well as the Citizen Army raised by James Connolly, head of the Irish Labour Party, had few seasoned or battle-tested men, but the men they had were brave and devoted to the cause. This, if ever, was the time.

Chapter 2

THE BEGINNING

WHAT IS KNOWN as the Easter Week rising of 1916 was well planned, and the British were completely unprepared for it. Yet before a shot was fired, the Irish rebel leaders at Liberty Hall in Dublin knew in their hearts that a military victory in this Easter Week rising was hopeless because of two things that had happened.

When stocky, bowlegged little James Connolly, in the dark green uniform of a commandant-general in the Irish Citizen Army, stepped briskly down the steps of Liberty Hall to march off his men, he half-whispered to one of his friends, "Bill, we're going out to be slaughtered."

Yet although Connolly and the other leaders knew they were going to be beaten, and that blood, sweat and suffering lay ahead, they felt sure that this first struggle was only the beginning. They might not survive to see it, but Ireland would gain freedom from the British shackles she had worn for centuries.

Groups of the rebels marched off to occupy strategic points in various parts of the city. What remained in front of Liberty Hall was only a pitifully small main rebel force—about 150 men lined up in shabby ranks, with two drays and a closed cab all jammed with arms, pickaxes, crowbars, sledgehammers and other equipment. The men were led by Padraic Pearse, the commander in chief, with his three commandants-general following—Connolly, Thomas MacDonagh of the Irish Volunteers and Joseph Plunkett. Plunkett, director of military operations, was dying of tuberculosis. He was just out of the hospital after a serious operation, and his throat was swathed in bandages.

Just as the rebels lined up, one of the touring cars then popular among automobile models drew up. Out of it leaped The O'Rahilly. A man directly descended from one of the ancient Irish clan chieftains, and the oldest member of his family, he had the privilege of using "The" instead of his given name before his last one.

The O'Rahilly was treasurer of the Irish Volunteers, but no one expected to see him. What he had been up to on a wild, all-night ride through the counties to the south was of no help to men like Padraic Pearse and James Connolly. The O'Rahilly had been trying to stop the uprising down there to the south. But now, seeing that in Dublin the rebellion *was* going to go on, he would fight—and fight with the most desperate courage almost to the end, when a British bullet cut him down. They cheered him and loaded his automobile with equipment too.

Now this main force marched off along the quays on the north bank of the murky, greenish, sluggishly flowing River Liffey, which cuts almost straight through the center of roughly circular Dublin like an equator. At the O'Connell Bridge, smack in the center of the business district, the rebels swung right, northward, up Sackville Street (today O'Connell Street), Dublin's widest, grandest thoroughfare.

The column, on the west side of Sackville Street, caused no excitement. People were used to seeing groups of the Citizen Army and the Irish Volunteers marching and drilling. Most of the pedestrians simply watched with idle curiosity. A great many Irishmen and Irishwomen took no interest in the talk of rebellion and freedom. They were resigned to living under British domination. Many women had husbands fighting with the British army in France against the Germans in World War I. They received money from England called "separation pay," and they wanted no rebellion to stop those checks coming.

Just as in the American Revolution, when thousands of Tories in the colonies supported Britain, so did thousands of the Irish in 1916. In front of the Metropole Hotel on the east side of Sackville Street, a few lounging British officers grinned at the motley rebel column across the way. A large number of British officers and soldiers were on leave this Easter week from their barracks throughout the city and suburbs, and from military headquarters in Dublin Castle.

The Irish column was approaching the General Post Office. It looks almost exactly the same on the outside today as it did then—a massive, granite building. James Connolly gave orders: "Company, halt! Left turn!" As the men obeyed: "The General Post Office—charge!"

The men broke ranks and rushed the building. Inside, it was much like any other large post office, with long counters of teakwood. The employees were busy with the receiving, sorting and dispatching of the mails. People were posting letters and packages and buying stamps. But all froze, motionless, when the horde of men burst in.

"Everybody out!" James Connolly shouted.

For a moment no one moved, too dazed with surprise to

obey. A woman's shrill voice demanded: "I want to buy some stamps!"

Then, looking into the muzzles of guns and seeing bayonets glitter, the people and the ground floor office staff made for the doors in a wild stampede.

Michael Collins, Plunkett's aide-de-camp, probably the toughest daredevil of all the men who fought in the Irish Rebellion, took charge of arrangements for turning the General Post Office into a formidable fortress.

"Smash the windows and barricade them!" he yelled. The men jumped gleefully to their task. From all over the ground floor came the crash and tinkle of glass under the impact of rifle butts. Other rebels moved heavy tables, chairs, desks and other furniture against the windows. Still others piled up books, ledgers and pads and squatted behind them for protection.

"We haven't seized the telegraph instrument room yet," The O'Rahilly told Pearse. A detachment sent scrambling up the stairs came face to face with the businesslike muzzles of seven rifles held by the Post Office guard. Not knowing the guns were not loaded, a Volunteer shot and wounded the sergeant of the guard, and the others threw down their weapons. The Volunteers' leader detailed one of his men to take the wounded guard to the hospital and the rest occupied the second floor of the Post Office.

James Connolly spoke to Captain Séan O'Kelly: "Séan, will you go over to Liberty Hall and bring me back a couple of flags?"

O'Kelly soon returned with one traditional green flag of Ireland with a harp on it and the words THE IRISH REPUBLIC in gold and white letters. And he had a second flag, a tricolor of green for Catholic southern Ireland, white for peace and orange for Protestant Northern Ireland, or Ulster—the same as the national flag of Ireland today, even though Northern Ireland remained a part of Britain.

They hoisted the flags to the roof of the General Post Office. People in Sackville Street gazed curiously up at them. They knew something was up, but they did not think it was anything serious. A rebellion or two not many years before had been quickly stamped out by the British.

Actually, this was different. This rebellion had been planned for months by Pearse, Connolly, Plunkett and other leaders of rebellious factions in Ireland. They had worked out every possible detail. This time, they had resolved, they would not fail.

The rebels' problem was to occupy certain locations in the city that would enable them to control it against the British garrisons in barracks scattered through the city and its suburbs, and also to control the roads and railway lines into the city over which British reinforcements might move.

The heart of the British government in Ireland was Dublin Castle, its original part built in the thirteenth century. It stood, and does today, in the heart of Dublin, south of the Liffey. In 1916 it was the residence of Lord Wimbourne, the Lord Lieutenant or British governor of Ireland; Sir Matthew Nathan, the under-secretary; and other high officials. The rebels hoped not only to seize it but first to cut it off completely from telephone and telegraph communications with any other part of the city, the rest of Ireland and London itself.

General headquarters for the rebels would be the General Post Office. One of the strategic outposts would be the Four Courts, a huge building just north of the Liffey and a little over half a mile west of the center of Dublin, the O'Connell

Bridge. In 1916 the Four Courts was the seat of the British high courts of justice in Ireland. After taking it, the rebels planned to establish small outposts in that general area as well.

Probably the most important post, strategically, would be at Boland's Bakery in the southeastern part of the city, also with outposts nearby. If reinforcements were sent to Ireland from England, they would undoubtedly land at Kingstown, on the coast just southeast of Dublin. The Boland's Bakery area controlled the railway and roads entering the city from that direction.

To keep British soldiers from coming in from barracks in the southwestern suburbs, the South Dublin Union, a workhouse, with outposts at Roe's and Jameson's distilleries, would be used as strong points.

There were two other Irish strong points. From Jacob's Biscuit Factory and its vicinity, troops could be prevented from entering from the south, especially from the large Portobello Barracks. It would be an outpost of a main force on St. Stephen's Green, then and today a beautiful park in central Dublin, south of the Liffey.

The Irish leaders had carefully collected information about the city's telephone and telegraph lines. They knew exactly where and how to cut the cables that would isolate Dublin Castle from its Irish barracks and garrisons, as well as the world.

On that Easter Monday, Commandant Edmund Kent stationed thirty-eight officers and men in the South Dublin Union and outposts. Kent had with him a man who was as ferocious a fighter as Michael Collins; unlike that burly giant, Cathal Brugha was a half-pint of a man, though he was every inch a tiger. At the Union and the outposts, the men put up barricades and other defenses.

Commandant Edward Daly of the First Volunteer Battalion was to seize and occupy the Four Courts. His force was all too small, but he sent Lieutenant Joseph MacGuiness with twenty men to occupy the building, then divided the rest into four small parties. They began erecting barricades in the streets surrounding the Four Courts. In nearby Church Street they seized a lorry, as motor trucks are called in Ireland, and heaved it over on its side, partly blocking the street. In another street they charged into houses and hauled out bedsteads for a barricade, ignoring the curses and frightful language of the Irish housewives of that slum district. In still another street they piled cobblestones into a barrier. Ahead of the barricades they scattered broken glass to stop cavalry charges.

At the mobilization point for the men to defend the highly important southeastern approaches, only thirty-five rebels had appeared by ten minutes to twelve that Easter Monday, and even the captain of this Volunteer company had not come. Nevertheless, Lieutenant Simon Donnelly marched them off in two sections. With twenty men he himself went to Boland's Bakery, where Commandant Eamon de Valera was stationed. The other fifteen men made their way to Upper Mount Street, close to where British reinforcements would probably approach the city. They included several of the bravest and boldest fighting men and best shots in the rebel army. All were to see some of the bloodiest fighting of the ill-fated rebellion, and their guns would do terrible damage to the British. In small parties they occupied houses and other positions that commanded the road and rail approaches to the city.

The main body of Joseph Connolly's Citizen Army was to occupy St. Stephen's Green with outposts, especially the one toward Portobello Barracks. Commanding this force was

Commandant Michael Mallin, another fearless, resourceful officer. Second in command was Countess Constance Markievicz.

A woman was the last person one would expect to see as second in command at strategic St. Stephen's Green—or anywhere else, for that matter. But the countess was no ordinary woman. She was tall, aristocratic-looking, and dark-haired, and wore a woolen blouse with brass buttons and tweed knee breeches, both dark green, and puttees. She had a cartridge belt jammed with bullets around her waist, with a small automatic pistol on one side and a wicked-looking Mauser rifle-pistol on the other. Completing this unusual uniform was a black velour hat trimmed with feathers.

She was Irish-born. Constance Gore Booth, daughter of a Protestant landowner in County Sligo, had married a Polish nobleman. Instead of being pro-British, as most such families were, Constance had become passionately devoted to Irish freedom. Now she was with the rebels in St. Stephen's Green, with some Red Cross nurses to look out for the needs of the men, and she was determined to fight and, if necessary, to die.

Thus the short-handed rebels were dispersed to await the onslaught that was sure to come. Even considering the Irish weakness in numbers, they were ready to give the unprepared British, whose country was already embroiled in the life-and-death struggle of World War I, such a fight that but for the two disastrous events already mentioned, and one almost as critical, the rebels might have won then and there.

Chapter 3

THE AUD and a
FUTILE JOURNEY

IN SOUTHERN IRELAND there is no wilder, rockier stretch of
coastline than that of Kerry, the southwesternmost county.
Long, narrow harbors reach far inland, with peninsulas between them. There are some fine, sandy beaches, but much
of this coast is forbidding, with frowning headlands at whose
feet the surf boils and crashes in. Villages are few and small.
A better place for a smuggler to land contraband cannot be
imagined.

At 4:15 P.M. on Holy Thursday, April 20, 1916, a ship
reached the tiny, uninhabited island of Inishtooskert in Tralee Bay. She appeared to be a nondescript freighter, probably
bound into Tralee. She flew the Norwegian ensign and had
large Norwegian flags painted on each side, as ships of neutral
nations did in those perilous days of the German submarines
in World War I. On her bow and stern was her name: AUD.

Dusk fell. From the *Aud*'s bridge Captain Karl Spindler
continually swept the sea and shore through binoculars. Not
seeing what he was looking for, he shook his head, puzzled.
At short intervals a sailor in the *Aud*'s bow displayed two
green lanterns and then put them out of sight. But Captain

Spindler, still looking for two green answering lights, saw only a few dim, twinkling white lights from shoreline hamlets. After steaming about for several hours, at 1:30 A.M. Captain Spindler anchored the *Aud* in the protecting lee of Inishtooskert Island.

The strange story of the *Aud* begins in Lübeck, Germany. She was actually the German freighter *Libau,* and Captain Spindler was a lieutenant in the German Navy. They had gone to great pains to make the *Aud* Norwegian in every detail. Her twenty-one officers and seamen even had Norwegian books and pictures of Norwegian girls and letters from them in their quarters. Their uniforms were those of Norwegian seamen, and even the buttons were stamped with the name of a company in Norway. The men spoke in a low-German dialect they hoped would pass for Norwegian.

Anyone looking under the hatches that covered the *Aud*'s holds would have seen a harmless-looking cargo of enameled steel ware, tin bathtubs, wooden doors and frames and similar general cargo carrying regular shipper's marks showing them bound for Genoa and Naples. On the top was a consignment of heavy planks—pit-props supposedly destined for the coal mines of Cardiff, Wales. But below this camouflage were 20,000 rifles, a million rounds of ammunition and ten machine guns.

There was only one important thing in which the *Aud* was not equipped. In those early days of radio she had none.

The German Admiralty knew better than to risk having the *Aud* thoroughly searched by British patrols in the English Channel. Captain Spindler headed her north over the far longer but safer route around the northern coast of Scotland and down the western coast of Ireland.

Nevertheless, the voyage was a perilous though lucky one.

The *Aud* managed to weather the worst gale Captain Spindler had ever experienced. The ship went as far north as the Arctic Circle and kept far to the west to avoid the British blockade. Several times British auxiliary cruisers overhauled the freighter and looked her over suspiciously, but let her proceed.

Another, entirely different vessel was involved in the *Aud*'s adventure. On April 12 the German submarine *U-19* left the great naval base at Kiel. She carried three passengers—Sir Roger Casement, Robert Monteith and another man known only as Bailey. The U-boat, taking the shorter route to Ireland, would rendezvous with the *Aud* in Tralee Bay on April 20.

Sir Roger Casement was born an Irishman, but entered the British consular service, where his career was so brilliant that he was knighted. Soon afterward, however, he returned to Ireland and became intensely interested in the cause of Irish freedom.

Casement believed that if Germany and her allies won World War I, Ireland could gain freedom from Britain. In September, 1914, he went to New York. There an Irish-American organization devoted to Irish freedom, the Clan na Gael, furnished the money to send Casement to Germany to gain her support.

The German high command realized that Irish freedom gained with their help would mean they could put troops into Ireland, establish naval bases at Irish ports and squeeze England between enemies on both sides. But when Casement told them what he wanted, they laughed.

Casement asked for a large expedition of German troops to drive the British out of Ireland, as well as 200,000 rifles and machine guns for a brigade of volunteers they had allowed him to recruit among Irish prisoners captured while with the British army in France. This man was either a dreamer or crazy, they decided, and began dealing directly with the Clan na Gael in New York. Under the deal they made, no German troops would be sent to Ireland and only 20,000 rifles in three ships.

Joseph Plunkett, knowing nothing of Casement's failure (he had even been unsuccessful in signing up more than fifty-two Irish prisoners in Germany for his brigade), sent him a secret dispatch saying that the rebellion was set for Easter Sunday. The big arms cargo would have to reach Tralee Bay not later than dawn on Good Friday. Casement was to bring German officers to help lead the uprising, and a German submarine had to be in Dublin harbor on Easter Sunday.

Casement replied with the true facts—a much smaller arms shipment than hoped for, positively no German officers, let alone troops, and no submarine in Dublin harbor. The German Foreign Office did not even bother to send out Casement's dispatch.

Another disappointment was in store for Sir Roger. The Germans broke their promise to send two trawlers with the arms shipment. One small freighter would make the voyage.

Casement was bitter against the Germans. Perhaps he suspected that Plunkett had not received his message. At all costs he would make sure the rebel chief of military operations knew what he could expect from Germany. He made a frantic plea to the Germans for a submarine to take him to Ireland. At last they let him go in the *U-19*.

At 2:30 A.M. on Good Friday, April 21, the submarine reached Tralee Bay. Her skipper also looked in vain for the two green signal lights ashore. The arrangement had been that when the green signals from the *Aud* were seen by rebels on shore, they would display two of their own, showing that all was clear for the landing of the arms.

There were no green lights ashore. The date of the uprising had been changed to Easter Monday. A message had been sent by way of New York to the German government saying that the arms must not be landed before the night of Easter Sunday. But since the *Aud* had no radio, Captain Spindler could not be notified.

Meanwhile, the *Aud* was in desperate trouble. The submarine did sight the freighter, but for some reason decided not to get in touch with her. Instead, the U-boat was brought to within two miles of a lonely stretch of beach, Banna Strand, north of the entrance to Tralee harbor. At 2:30 A.M. a collapsible boat carrying Sir Roger Casement and his two companions was lowered away. Each man had a lifebelt and a kit containing a Mauser pistol, a pair of binoculars and a sheath knife.

The submarine then got out as fast as possible, and with good reason. British intelligence had known vaguely of the plan for some time. The admiral in command of the British naval base at Queenstown (now renamed Cobh) had sent out some small warships to intercept the *Aud* off the western coast of Ireland. That had failed, but he also had a swarm of trawlers and other small armed craft searching every harbor and inlet. That was what had got the *Aud* into trouble.

At dawn on Good Friday the armed British trawler *Setter II* sighted the *Aud* at anchor, came alongside and hailed her: "What are you doing there?"

Captain Spindler was in a tight spot, but he decided to bluff it out. "Engine trouble," he shouted back.

"Stand by to be boarded," came the British reply.

The officer in charge of the boarding party demanded:

"Let's see your papers, Captain, and we want a look at your cargo."

The *Aud*'s faked documents, showing her to be of Norwegian registry, were in order, of course. And when the hatch covers were removed, the boarding officer was satisfied with the pile of pit-props he saw there, helping to conceal the *Aud*'s real cargo. The trawler went on her way.

Early that afternoon, however, the commanding officer of the British trawler *Lord Henage* received an alert about a suspicious ship in Tralee Bay. This time, when Spindler sighted the enemy ship, he decided to run for it. The anchor came up and on the *Aud*'s bridge the engine telegraph jangled to FULL AHEAD, and Spindler rang up the chief engineer.

"Get every knot you can out of her or we'll be sunk!" he shouted.

The decrepit *Aud* plunged ahead at the best speed she could make. The *Lord Henage* was already firing at long range. Then the chief engineer climbed to the bridge. "We can't maintain this speed or the boilers will burst!" he reported.

The *Lord Henage* had radioed for help. Two armed sloops, the *Zinnia* and *Bluebell,* soon loomed over the horizon. Meanwhile, the British Admiralty sent out an order: "If *Aud* is sighted, she is to be brought into port for examination."

It was all up with the *Aud*. British craft began to converge on her from every point of the compass. Captain Spindler cheated the British, however. He allowed the *Aud* to be escorted toward Queenstown, but just outside the harbor, and across the channel to block it if he could, he blew her up. She and her precious cargo sank in ten minutes, but the crew got off and Spindler lived to write two accounts of the

hair-raising adventures of the *Aud,* the *U-19* and Sir Roger
Casement.

By this time Casement's adventures were over, too. In the
darkness he and his companions had rowed for what seemed
like hours through the darkness without a sign of land ahead,
and the sea had become rough. Suddenly a white-topped
curler struck the little boat and capsized it. Luckily, they
were only about two hundred yards offshore, and thanks to
their life jackets they reached the beach. Casement collapsed
on the sand, gasping for breath.

They tried to find a hiding place until they could get in
touch with rebel friends. They were unable to sink the collapsible boat and had to leave it while they staggered on up
the beach.

About dawn an early-rising farmer found the boat. Along
the beach he came upon a sheath knife, then a box of ammunition and finally three loaded revolvers and the foot-
prints of three men. The farmer then made for the nearest
police station.

Searchers found Sir Roger Casement where his companions
had had to leave him, exhausted, in an ancient, abandoned
fort on Banna Strand.

This was one of the two grave events that doomed the
uprising to failure before it began. Yet, serious as it was, the
rebellion still might have succeeded but for the second disastrous occurrence just before the rising started.

To call Eóin MacNeill a troublemaker because he was responsible for the second disastrous event is unfair. He did
what he thought was right, and he was right as far as the
result of the Easter Week uprising was concerned.

MacNeill was a scholarly man, professor of early Irish

history at University College in Dublin, deeply devoted to the cause of Irish freedom. At the time of the rising he was chief of staff of the Irish Volunteers and its actual head. Thus, when he issued an order to the Volunteers, it was to be obeyed.

MacNeill was opposed to the rebellion from the time it was first planned. He did not believe it could succeed. Aware of his views, the other leaders kept their plans secret from him. When the first mobilization order for Easter Sunday was issued by Pearse, MacNeill thought it was just another of the parades and drills the rebel organizations often held. But on the night of Holy Thursday he learned that the order had gone out all over the country and it meant armed rebellion.

In a fury, MacNeill rushed to Padraic Pearse's house, roused him from bed and demanded to know what was going on. Pearse told him the truth. In spite of his blazing anger, MacNeill argued earnestly that the rising would fail.

"I feel that I am right," was the only answer he could get from Pearse.

"I will do everything I can to stop this, everything except to ring up Dublin Castle," MacNeill told him, and then stormed off.

The next morning MacDonagh and another leader, Séan MacDermott, went to see MacNeill. They told him that a German ship loaded with arms was on her way to Ireland. And anyhow, it was too late to stop the rising. With that, in spite of his feeling that the rebellion was doomed even with the help of the German guns, MacNeill agreed not to order it canceled.

What happened then is best seen through the eyes of Nora Connolly, the eldest of James Connolly's four daughters. Ireland is famous for pretty girls, and Nora was a lovely colleen. She was also intelligent, enterprising and self-reliant. Once she was old enough, she worked side by side with her father for Irish freedom.

While Nora was in Northern Ireland working with *Cumann na mBan,* or League of Women, in Belfast, James Connolly wrote her a letter showing how much reliance and trust he placed in her. A young, able Irish officer, Liam Mellows, had been deported to England and was required to lead the uprising against the British in County Galway. Nora's father asked her, with some of her companions, to rescue Mellows and bring him back to Ireland.

It was no safe or easy task, but it was accomplished. They took a roundabout route through Scotland and into the "Black Country" of England's Midlands, with its coal mines and industry, stopping only at safe addresses furnished by Nora's father. They located Mellows, took him into Scotland, disguised him as a priest and smuggled him back to Ireland.

From Dublin, James Connolly wrote his wife in Belfast, saying, "Tell Nora I am proud of her." He had good reason to be.

In April, 1916, with preparations for the uprising approaching a climax, Mrs. Connolly left Belfast on Good Friday with the two youngest of her daughters to be with her husband in Dublin. The two older girls, Nora and Agna, stayed in Belfast. On Saturday they went to a place in County Tyrone where a force of Irish soldiers was gathering in a drill hall.

"When do you mobilize?" Nora asked one of the men.

"Tomorrow morning." he replied. "We are waiting for the Belfast division to join us here."

Just then someone came into the hall, calling, "Miss Connolly, come outside! I have a message for you."

Mystified, she went out. The message was that Eóin Mac-

Neill had issued an order that there would be no fighting in Northern Ireland, demobilizing the Irish troops there.

Nora was stunned, realizing that this could ruin the chances of the rebellion's success. She took a night train for Dublin to let her father know. Arriving at five on Easter Sunday morning, she went immediately to the headquarters in Liberty Hall.

A sentry stopped her at the door, and she had some trouble in reaching her father. He had not gone to bed till three that morning and was asleep. But at last she convinced the guards she had to see him at once.

James Connolly arose at her knock. "What are you doing here?" he demanded when she told him who it was.

"Let me in, father," Nora said. "I am afraid there is something wrong." Inside, she told him what she had heard in Tyrone. "What does it mean?" she asked. "Are we not going to fight?"

"Not fight!" James Connolly cried. "Nora, if we don't fight now, we are disgraced forever."

"Then why were we told last night there would be no fighting in the North?" Nora asked.

"That is a different story from what we were told."

"Mine is the true one," she insisted.

Other leaders were called in, including Padraic Pearse. Nora got breakfast for those who had not eaten. One of the girls who were with Nora brought in a newspaper, the *Irish Independent,* and showed James Connolly a front-page item that read:

> Owing to the critical situation, all Volunteer parades and maneuvers are cancelled.
> > By order,
> > Eóin MacNeill

"What does this mean?" Connolly cried.

"Let me see it," said Pearse. "I know nothing whatsoever about this."

What had happened was that the news of the *Aud's* destruction had reached Eóin MacNeill Friday night. At first he decided it was too late to do anything, but on Saturday morning he changed his mind, issued the canceling order, had it sent by couriers to Cork, Belfast and Limerick and put the notice in the Dublin Sunday paper.

The seven chief rebel leaders in Dublin held a solemn council. They decided the rebellion should go on, but would be postponed until the following day, Easter Monday. Thomas MacDonagh put their combined feelings about canceling the rising into one short sentence: "We would be a disgrace to our generation."

On that fateful Easter Monday morning, Nora Connolly and the girls who had come with her from Tyrone were told they would be given a message to carry back to Northern Ireland as soon as Padraic Pearse signed it.

Nora's father came out of the council room in Liberty Hall carrying a large poster. He said to one of the girls, "Come here and read this carefully. It would be dangerous to allow you to carry it with you, but tell the men of the North what you have read."

He spread the poster on the table. It was headed:

THE PROVISIONAL GOVERNMENT
OF THE
IRISH REPUBLIC

"Irishmen and Irishwomen," it began. "In the name of God and of the dead generations from which she receives her old tradition of nationhood, Ireland, through us, summons her children to her flag and strikes for her freedom."

It was the Irish Declaration of Independence. It proclaimed an Irish Republic, guaranteeing religious and civil liberty to all, and declared Ireland free and independent.

Upon the young shoulders of Nora Connolly rested the responsibility for persuading the Northern Irish troops to disregard Eóin MacNeill's order and fight for freedom. She and her companions took a train out of Dublin that morning. But when they reached Tyrone, they found that most of the troops had already obeyed MacNeill's order. Nora did what she could, sending messages to the secret headquarters of Irish troops in Northern Ireland, saying that those in Dublin intended to fight and urging them to do the same.

Some were ready to fight. That night, in a pouring rain, Nora and the other girls were led through the darkness over a muddy road to a large barn. In this secret place, soldiers were waiting for orders to march. Nora and her companions were taken to a nearby farmhouse, where they spent the night. For three days they waited, but the marching order did not come.

Nora decided that she had to return to Dublin and warn her father and the other leaders there that they could expect little if any help from Northern Ireland. She sent the other girls back to Belfast and started out, walking, to pick up her sister Agna, who had gone to Carrickmore with the message from Dublin.

That evening, when Nora reached the farm where Agna was supposed to be, her sister had left with a dispatch for the village of Clogher. The farm had been raided by the British that afternoon. The searching party had discovered three thousand rounds of ammunition hidden in the peat stack.

That night the British search party returned. Nora had gone to bed, but they burst in, questioned her sharply and searched her suitcase and other belongings. Fortunately, they did not get her out of bed, where she had hidden a hundred rounds of ammunition and her revolver. Nor did they do so when they returned a third time late that night. The farm people were frightened out of their wits and ordered Nora to leave, but she refused to go until it was dawn.

The farm people said it was five miles to Clogher. Actually, it was fifteen. It was very warm for April. Nora had on a tweed skirt and raincoat over her uniform and was lugging her suitcase. For two miles the road ran through flatlands with no shade from the blazing sun. Then it passed through some of the boggy country with which Ireland abounds. Nora had passed no streams or springs and was so thirsty that she drank some of the stagnant bog water, hoping it was safe. When she reached the mountains that loomed ahead, she was too tired to enjoy the shade their forest offered. She sat down by the roadside, so exhausted that she didn't know how she was going to get up again.

Just then, down the road, she saw two girls coming toward her on bicycles. She gave a cry of joy and staggered to her feet. One of the cyclists was her sister Agna.

Before reaching Clogher the girls got food and tea. In the village they stayed overnight at the home of Agna's companion. In the morning the two sisters took a train to Dundalk, on the main line to Dublin. But there they learned that only military trains were running and knew the rising in Dublin must have begun.

Nora was terribly worried. Somehow she *had* to reach Dublin and warn her father and the others. "There's only one thing for it," she said. "We'll have to walk."

Neither knew that it was fifty-four miles to Dublin. As they started out, they saw a barricade across the road ahead— a real peril, for both girls had uniforms under their coats and skirts and Nora her revolver and ammunition. But luck was with them. The corporal's guard of British soldiers at the barrier smiled and let the girls pass, thinking they were two pretty country colleens returning from market in Dundalk.

As night approached, they realized they dared not register at a hotel or even ask for shelter at a country cottage where the people might not be rebel sympathizers. So they went down a path that branched off the road and climbed over a hedge and found themselves in a sheltered dell covered with grass and heather. They picked out a soft spot and settled down, supperless, for the night.

Ireland's climate is especially chilly and damp at night. A heavy mist settled over the field, and it grew colder and colder. Nora and Agna snuggled down as close together as possible, but both shivered and their teeth chattered. Through what seemed like an endless night neither one closed an eye.

Stiff and sore from the night's ordeal, they pushed on for the large town of Drogheda the next morning, Sunday. Perhaps there might be a local train going at least part of the way to Dublin.

In Drogheda the famished girls looked for a restaurant, but they were all closed. At the railroad station the answer was still: "Only military trains running."

Soon after leaving Drogheda they passed a signpost that said: "Dublin, 25 miles." By now their ordeal was beginning to tell on them. Agna had rubbed liniment on the soles of their feet, but it burned and they could hardly walk.

Reaching a plowed field, they took off their shoes and stockings and plunged their feet into the deliciously cool brown earth. It felt so good that both dozed off.

A sudden sound brought them both upright. That dull booming to the south could only be cannon fire from Dublin, now about eighteen miles away.

They hurried on. Then, to their consternation, another barricade of country carts loomed up ahead of them. They could see British soldiers searching the bicycles of two cyclists and their pockets as well. The girls knew a search would mean certain arrest for them. What made it worse was that just beyond the barrier stood a restaurant. They had had nothing to eat for more than twenty-four hours.

Once more luck was with them. Two boys who had come up to the barricade refused to be searched. The soldiers seized them, and while the boys struggled the two girls sneaked through the barricade and into the restaurant. The greatest peril of their journey was behind them.

Nora and Agna ate like two ravenous young wolves. The waitress hung about, and at last she said, "Are you coming from Dublin? I thought you might have some news."

"No," said Nora. "Have you heard how things are going there?"

"I heard they were surrendering in Dublin—that they were beaten," the girl replied.

While they were still about fifteen miles from Dublin, Nora's right leg gave out and she could no longer walk on it. But luck was still with them. A man and woman in a big touring car picked them up and carried them nearly to Clontarf, only a little north of Dublin. The man had only ominous news.

"People who live on the outskirts of Dublin can get no

supplies in the city," he said. "I've just been to Drogheda for bread."

Approaching the city after their ride, they saw a large British force of infantry, cavalry, artillery and supply wagons. "They're going to County Wexford," an old man told them. "They're going to try to drive out the rebels, who've captured two or three towns." He spat after them. "God curse them!"

At seven that night they reached the home of friends in the northern suburb of Drumconda.

"What is the news?" was the first thing Nora asked.

"The boys are beaten. They've all surrendered. They're all prisoners. The city has been burning since Thursday."

Nora was so stunned that she could only cry, "My father?"

"He's wounded and was taken a prisoner to Dublin Castle. They don't think he'll live. Though God knows, maybe they'll all be killed."

And that was the tragic news that greeted Nora Connolly at the end of her futile journey.

Chapter 4

THE FIRST ACTION

News of the *Aud's* destruction reached Dublin Castle on Holy Saturday, April 22. With that, Lord Wimbourne made up his mind to arrest the Sinn Fein leaders. Nothing was done about it at once, however. The Lord Lieutenant was smugly satisfied that the *Aud* had carried with her to the bottom of Queenstown harbor all immediate hopes of the uprising which had been rumored as soon to happen.

On Easter Monday, however, at about noon, a group of Wimbourne's chief officials was meeting in an office at the castle to decide how to carry out the arrests. They had no feeling of any great hurry about it. The *Aud* was gone, and the notice in the *Irish Independent* signed by MacNeill had canceled all "maneuvers" set for Easter Sunday.

At about the same time, Constable James O'Brien, on duty at the main gate, pooh-poohed a Red Cross nurse returning to duty in the castle when she asked, "Is it true that the Sinn Feiners are going to take the castle?" Minutes later he was dead.

At that noon hour of Monday, April 24, the editor of the Dublin *Mail and Express* looked out of his office window across the street from the castle at a shout from one of his staff. At the main gate was a small group of men and women in dark green uniforms, with slouch hats pinned up on one side with the badge of the Transport Union, a red hand. They were armed. Constable O'Brien tried to stop them at the gate. They shot him down.

Inside the gate a sentry fired his rifle into the air to alert his mates in the guard room and fled for cover. The Irish rebels then burst into the Upper Castle Yard.

At the conference over the Sinn Fein arrests, Major Ivor Price, the military intelligence officer, heard the shots and dashed out of the office. In the Upper Yard he saw half a dozen rebels breaking into the guard room. He emptied his revolver at them, but his aim was bad and he retreated.

There were just six soldiers in the guard room, heating stew for their lunch. When they heard the shots, they seized their rifles and started for the door. A homemade bomb came hurtling through the window and exploded, killing no one but stunning them long enough for the rebels to seize and tie them up with their own puttees.

Had the rebels known the true situation, they might have captured Dublin Castle then and there. Their six prisoners and the sentry were the only soldiers on duty in the castle that holiday Easter Monday. The nearest reinforcements were lolling about in the Ship Street Barracks across the street—and there were only twenty-five soldiers there. But the rebel leader withdrew his force; he put some in a nearby shop and others in the newspaper office, while he and the main force took over the then unoccupied City Hall close by. And within a short time strong reinforcements—180 British of the Royal Irish Rifles and the Dublin Fusileers— moved into the castle through the Ship Street entrance.

When Major Price found he could round up only twenty-
five men at the Ship Street Barracks, he picked up the telephone to call army headquarters near Phoenix Park. The
line was dead.

Most of the rebels who had been ordered to cut the telephone cables had done their jobs perfectly. But their attempt
to destroy a telephone junction through which all the Irish
military lines ran failed, and the man who was to cut off
practically all the regular Dublin lines did not show up. Here
was the third disaster that helped to seal the fate of the Easter
uprising. Thus it was possible for Dublin Castle to summon
reinforcements from the outlying barracks and, in a little
over an hour after the rebellion began, to arrange for flashing word of it to London by radio.

While Commandant Edward Daly's slim First Volunteer
Battalion was seizing and occupying the Four Courts and
setting up outposts, a mounted troop of Lancers of the British
Cavalry Sixth Reserve Regiment started out from the Marl-
borough Barracks in Phoenix Park at the west end of Dublin.
The Lancers clattered through the streets to the railway
terminal just north of the Liffey near where it empties into
the harbor at the opposite end of town. Their mission had
nothing to do with any expected trouble; it was simply to
escort five carts loaded with rifles, rifle grenades and bombs
to the barracks.

Just after most of the rebel detachments had marched off
from Liberty Hall, the British cavalry and the wagons passed
it. The horsemen would have been perfect targets, but the
officer in charge of those still at Liberty Hall had orders to
avoid any action until the rebel units had occupied their
posts around the city. So the convoy passed Liberty Hall, and

also O'Connell Bridge, where rebel scouts let them go by.

Just beyond the bridge, Bachelor's Walk runs along the north side of the river. There a man shouted to the Lancers, "Look out for yourselves! The Sinn Feiners are out. They're up ahead!"

The Lancers' commander thought the fellow was trying to annoy them with a false alarm, and the convoy kept on. On the way they would pass the Four Courts. From one of the outposts at Church Street, just beyond the huge building, the rebels saw the British first. They knelt in the road and gave the Lancers a volley that, probably because the Irish were so astonished, was not too accurate. Nevertheless, several of the cavalrymen had their horses shot from under them.

The lieutenant in charge of the Lancers wheeled his mount. "Get into a side street!" he shouted, and the troops scattered. Some spurred their horses toward one of the gates to the Four Courts. A rebel guard there opened fire on them, but missed, and the riders galloped on past. The British lieutenant led another group of his men toward an open space east of the Four Courts, but a hail of fire drove them back. Order and discipline among the panic-stricken Lancers had vanished, but the lieutenant did a remarkable job of rallying those near him. They found shelter in a building across from the Four Courts, barricaded the windows and, when no attack came, dragged the boxes of munitions off the carts and inside with them.

Many others of the scattered troop were wounded or had their horses shot and were taken prisoner. Two riders swung wildly into Church Street and met another volley that missed them. But as they charged on, two rebel officers shot one Lancer dead and wounded the other.

They took the dead man's lance to the corner of Church

and North King streets, a couple of blocks north of the Four
Courts, stuck it into a manhole in the middle of the street
and triumphantly fastened the tricolored flag of the new
Irish Republic to it.

In this first real engagement the rebels had drawn first
blood.

Commandant Kent and his vice-commandant, the fiery Cathal Brugha, could have used far more than the small force
of Volunteers they marched to the South Dublin Union. The
grounds of the Union were large and were surrounded by a
high wall, and there were a number of buildings. Kent detailed thirty-eight officers and men to occupy the buildings.
He divided the rest of his force into small groups and placed
them where they could intercept British troops coming in
from the southwestern suburbs in case they did not take the
main route passing the Union.

Lieutenant William Cosgrave pointed out something:
"You can't hope to hold the whole Union with the men you
have. Why not use the Nurses' Home? It's the strongest building, and it's located where we can control the most important
approaches." Kent agreed, and the windows of the three-
story, stone Nurses' Home were smashed and barricaded.

From their outpost, Lieutenant William O'Brien and his
little force first saw the enemy approaching over the main
road. He lifted his head above the cover they had taken and
saw about twenty khaki-clad figures coming over an elevation
in the road about three hundred yards away, their glittering
bayonets fixed.

Another outpost—four Volunteers under Section Commander John Joyce—was nearer, behind a wall only about
150 yards away from the British force, which totaled two

hundred soldiers of the Royal Irish Regiment. They had halted while the twenty advance men moved forward slowly, deploying across the road.

Joyce's men gave the advance detachment a volley that felled three of the enemy. The rest made for cover, now running, now crouching. The British sergeant in charge of them stood coolly with his back to the Volunteers, disdaining danger while he directed his men to cover in houses beside the road. Joyce tried to pick the sergeant off, but the Englishman kept shifting about, and each time Joyce's bullet missed. But his men brought down several more of the enemy.

Again the Irish had drawn first blood, but their own would flow soon enough. The British, using the cover of the elevation in the road, kept up a continuous fire for two hours, and the Volunteers at these advance outposts were finally driven to take cover in the Nurses' Home.

The British then began an assault on the Union grounds from both front and rear. As the main force hurled itself against a small wooden door beside the locked southern entrance, the Rialto Gate, Captain James Murphy and his little force in nearby Jameson's Distillery poured on a withering fire. British soldiers trying to scale the wall were picked off, and an officer who got his leg over the wall was shot off and fell dead to the ground. But at last the greatly superior numbers of the British began to tell. The Volunteers at the Rialto Gate had to surrender, and the enemy stormed into the Union grounds.

This battle the British had won. But dislodging the Volunteers holed up in the Nurses' Home would be a different story.

Commandant Eamon de Valera, in command at Boland's Bakery, was a strange person indeed, yet destined for greatness. He was born in America in 1882, on Lexington Avenue between 51st and 52nd streets in New York City. Today tall buildings rise everywhere in this teeming part of the great city, and subway trains rumble below Lexington Avenue. But Eamon remembered nothing of his early days in New York. His Spanish father died when Eamon was less than three years old, and his mother took him back to her native Ireland.

Eamon resembled his dark and swarthy father. He had a proud and piercing look, but far from being fierce, de Valera was at heart a gentle, kindly man. He was not a professional soldier, but a professor of mathematics passionately devoted to the struggle for Irish freedom. There seemed little of the distinguished leader about him, for he was a man of few words. A great worrier, he changed his mind about his military plans too often and did not have the magnetism that draws men to follow some leaders through any sort of danger. Yet no officer in the rebellion gave more thought to the comfort and safety of his men.

What marked de Valera most of all for greatness was his political ability and his steady devotion to the cause of Irish freedom, refusing to compromise on anything short of full freedom from Britain. In this desperate fight in southeastern Dublin, de Valera does not stand out strongly except for his dogged determination to fight to the last. The great heroes were his officers and men at the outposts.

Once the force in Boland's Bakery was established, with de Valera's own headquarters in a small dispensary next door, he set up the outposts, not only to protect him from the nearby Beggars Bush Barracks, from which he feared an attack—actually needlessly—but, in the opposite direction, to block reinforcements from England landing at Kingstown from reaching the city.

Boland's Bakery fronted on Grand Canal Street. The Grand Canal makes a sweep roughly in a half circle from west to east, curving through southern Dublin before joining the Liffey. De Valera had some of the bakery's bread vans hauled to the bridge at Grand Canal Street and their wheels removed, blocking one of the main routes to the heart of Dublin.

His next concern was to seal off the railway line from Kingstown that ran past the bakery on an embankment, as well as the main road from there over which enemy reinforcements would march if they could not use the railway. Some of his men ripped up the rails with sledgehammers, while others smashed signal mechanisms.

As for the outposts south of the bakery, closer to where troops from Kingstown would come, Lieutenant Michael Malone, Section-Commander James Grace and fifteen men occupied a terraced mansion at 25 Northumberland Road on the corner of Haddington Road. Its residents, sympathetic to Sinn Fein, had left. In what was to follow two days later, No. 25, Mick Malone and Grace were to be concerned in great deeds.

Handsome, fair-haired, quiet and serious-minded young Mick didn't look like a fighter—but he matched other heroes of the Irish rebel army in daring and bravery, and there was no better shot among them. De Valera had given Malone his own Mauser rifle-pistol because Mick had only a single-shot, nonrepeating rifle.

Section-Commander George Reynolds took over Clanwilliam House, close to the Mount Street Bridge over the Grand Canal. Like 25 Northumberland Road, Clanwilliam House and the brave rebels who defended it were to be the center of a furious fight against the enemy.

Next morning, Tuesday, Mick Malone managed to get four reinforcements from de Valera at Boland's Bakery for Clanwilliam House, bringing the garrison there to seven men. The new ones also brought eight assorted rifles and three revolvers, along with two thousand extra rounds of ammunition.

At Boland's Bakery the men were in high spirits. They had heard a totally false report that the Germans had landed troops in Ireland and were marching for Dublin. But de Valera's look was more ominous and worried than ever; he had slept little if at all, and his eyes were red-rimmed and wild-looking. He had good cause to worry. Little had happened yet, but it would, soon enough.

Commandant Michael Mallin knew that it would not be easy to hold St. Stephen's Green, but it had to be held if possible. Ten streets funneled into it, three of them main routes that reinforcements coming from south of Dublin might use. Mallin saw that his force there could become easy targets from some of the houses surrounding the square. He, Countess Markievicz and a small detachment seized several of them, smashed and barricaded the windows and left snipers there. All traffic was then stopped, and draymen, motorists, cab drivers and tramway men were forced to block the four streets surrounding the square with their vehicles.

Mallin made one serious mistake. He did not seize the Shelbourne Hotel on the north side, or the adjoining United Services Club.

The Shelbourne, nearly a hundred years old in 1916, was then, as today, one of Dublin's distinguished hotels. Its famous Long Bar and its restaurant were crowded that noonday with British officers and well-to-do guests. Afterward, a good-sized group of officers and gentlemen up from the country for a horse show at suburban Ballsbridge were astonished and irate when Mallin's men promptly took them prisoner. What did these shoddy-looking ruffians mean by this? Most of the civilians were soon released, but the rebels held on to the officers.

As night fell there was almost no activity around St. Stephen's Green, but at about four the next morning, Tuesday, a steady rat-tat-tat broke the city's quiet. It came from the Shelbourne. British troops had crept in and occupied it and the United Services Club next door.

Too late, Michael Mallin regretted not having seized the two buildings. In a three-hour battle one rebel was killed and a number wounded. From the shallow trench where she lay, Countess Markievicz twice silenced a British machine gun with well-aimed shots from her rifle-pistol. But by 6 A.M. Mallin saw that holding the Green would only mean sacrificing his men. The fearless countess crawled over the grass to give other rebel positions Mallin's order: "Withdraw to the Cuffe Street southwest corner."

There, even though the position was protected by trees, shrubbery and a mound of earth, the machine gun fire was too hot. Just across the street from the west gate was the Royal College of Surgeons. It offered good protection, and its windows and roof excellent positions for sharpshooters. Although under fire, the force and the Red Cross nurses with them made it safely across the street. Behind them on the Green lay the bodies of five dead rebels.

A fair-sized crowd gathered in front of the General Post Office heard Padraic Pearse, standing at the main entrance with James Connolly by his side, read the Declaration of Independence. For all the response Pearse got from them, he could have been reading from the telephone book. The people there understood little of what it would mean for their future, and couldn't have cared less.

But James Connolly, his face aglow with joy, shook the commander in chief's hand when he had finished and said, "Thanks be to God, Pearse, that we have lived to see this day!"

Soon a much larger crowd filled Sackville Street, O'Connell Bridge and across it at the corner of D'Olier and Westmoreland streets, as the news of the General Post Office occupation spread. They were waiting to see the British strike.

Inside the Post Office the rebels were fidgety. At each of the many false alerts of an attack, itchy-fingered rebels fired their rifles or shotguns.

The mob increased. Women drawing separation pay hurled insults at the rebels, who hurled them right back. A number of fights broke out between "shawlies"—women of the slums who wore shawls on their heads and shoulders. Suddenly a line of priests with their hands linked spread across Sackville Street, sweeping the mob before it down toward O'Connell Bridge. But when the wave had advanced to Lord Admiral Nelson's towering monument in the middle of the street above the Post Office, the mob broke through, scattering the priests like so many blackbirds. Then the crowd itself scattered as a shout went up: "The Lancers! The Lancers!"

At this cry there was a tumult of shouted orders in the General Post Office as the men grabbed their weapons. Above the pandemonium came Pearse's voice: "Don't fire till I give the command! Let them gallop the full length of the building!"

The troop of Lancers had halted momentarily at the head of Sackville Street. They were a magnificent sight, erect on their beautifully groomed, high-spirited horses and holding their long, sharp-tipped lances. Their commanding colonel's gaze swept Sackville Street arrogantly; the mob was disappearing toward the bridge, save for the daring ones who took up observation posts they hoped would be safe from bullets.

At that moment a company of Volunteers from Rathfarnham, just south of Dublin, arrived, late but ready for battle. They reached an entrance to the Post Office just as the Lancers began a quick trot toward them. The desperate newcomers shouted to be let in.

"Who are you?" came the challenge from inside.

"We're from Rathfarnham! For God's sake, open up!"

"Break the blasted windows and inside with you, you bloody fools!" came the reply. The Volunteers found a couple of windows still unbarricaded and loopholed, and tumbled inside with moments to spare.

There in the Post Office, disregarding Pearse's orders, excited rebels gave the British cavalry a scattering volley. Seasoned fighters, trained to fire accurately, might have wiped out the Lancers completely. Four of them fell dying from their horses, and the troop was thrown into disorder. But the colonel, sword flashing, rode about madly among the milling, wheeling Lancers and forced them back up Sackville Street to a safe position.

He had had enough, and did not order another charge. Thus, in spite of no battle experience and disregard of orders, these Irish defenders too had gained a small victory. They had lost one man, almost certainly killed accidentally by a bullet from a rebel sniper post across the street.

Meanwhile, from the back streets that were the worst slums in Europe except for those of Naples, the poor swarmed into Sackville Street. They were ragged, dirty and verminous; some were barefoot. They smashed the plate-glass windows of luxurious shops and looted them of hats, shoes, other clothing—everything they could lay their hands on. An exclusive confectioner's shop was sacked, and the looters stuffed themselves with expensive candies. For these poverty-stricken wretches, the rebellion meant only a chance to obtain beautiful, warm clothing and other luxuries they had never dreamed of having.

By the evening of the 24th, British reinforcements from outlying barracks had reached central Dublin in spite of the rebels' efforts to stop them, and more were making their way against stiff opposition. There were now a thousand troops in Dublin Castle alone, and plans were made to rout the rebels out of their strong position in nearby City Hall, occupied after the failure to take the castle. Late that evening a machine gun set up in a concealed position began spraying a stream of bullets at City Hall.

The rebels' situation there quickly became desperate. Bullets crashed through the windows and ricocheted from wall to wall of the rooms inside. Plaster fell and whole walls collapsed in clouds of dust.

A hundred British troops tried to storm the building but were driven back by a storm of fire from a few rebels behind the barricades they had set up outside. A second assault party advanced far enough to be caught in a hail of bullets from rebels on the roof of the newspaper office opposite the main gate, and had to retreat, leaving twenty men in the road, most of them dead.

Again the British attacked. On the roof of the City Hall, rebels fired down on them so fast that they had to wrap handkerchiefs around their overheated rifle barrels, and their faces were blackened by burned gunpowder. But hand grenades, thrown through the holes where windows had been by troops who had advanced through the City Hall cellars, had a deadly effect.

The second assault wave came on again. It burst into the building, forcing the Irish defenders on the ground floor up the stairs to the first landing. For a time their murderous volleys forced the attackers back. But more British poured in. The heroic defenders on the stairs were wiped out.

The attackers swarmed up the stairway. On the roof the rebels heard a shout in the darkness: "Surrender in the name of the King!" The Irish paid no attention but battled through the night without sleep. When dawn came, after first one and then a second Irish commander there had been killed, and British troops storming through the skylight overwhelmed them, they surrendered. Yet across the street in the shop and newspaper offices, the rebels refused demands to surrender with defiant shouts.

Chapter 5

THE BLOODY DAYS

IN THE MISTY dawn of Wednesday, April 26, a grayish shape nudged up the Liffey and anchored off the Custom House. The *Helga* was a little converted fisheries patrol vessel. A shell from a first-class warship could have blown her out of the water. But the *Helga* was well fitted for what she had come to do, for she mounted a one-pounder naval gun and several machine guns.

The British thought Liberty Hall, close to the Custom House, was still occupied by the rebels. Actually, only a caretaker was there, and he escaped before the *Helga*'s bombardment quickly made a shell out of the building. The rebels suffered no casualties—but the thunder of the gun, the screech of the shells and the constant hail of machine gun fire put fear into the hearts of more than one of those holding the General Post Office just up Sackville Street.

Then a still greater menace appeared. For all their painstaking planning, the rebel leaders had overlooked the important strategic point of Trinity College, south of the Liffey, only half a mile from the General Post Office, its roof commanding all of lower Sackville Street. The British took

59

prompt advantage of the rebel mistake and seized the college. A continuous chatter of machine gun fire began to rain down on lower Sackville Street.

The most important result was that a radio transmitter, rigged up by the rebels with the greatest ingenuity and difficulty in a building there, was cut off. It had continually been broadcasting messages announcing the new Irish Republic over a much-used wavelength, and requesting that the announcement be relayed to other stations.

A worse catastrophe struck the Irish that Wednesday. On Tuesday night the first units of an entire British division had reached Kingstown, and on Wednesday morning they headed for the city. Unless by some miracle they could be prevented from reaching central Dublin, they had the power to crush the rebellion quickly and totally. Stopping one of the columns was the all-but-hopeless task that fell to Commandant Eamon de Valera and his skimpy force in and around Boland's Bakery.

This British column took the coastal route that led to the Mount Street Bridge over the Grand Canal. The soldiers were from Nottinghamshire and were called the Sherwood Foresters or Robin Hoods, since the forest where the fabled outlaw and his merry men lived was in that county. The Robin Hoods were not going to have the sport their namesake had in robbing the rich to help the poor and outwitting the sheriff of Nottingham. But considering that they were raw young recruits who had never been in battle, they underwent a frightfully bloody ordeal with great credit.

About noon, while the advance force of the British column was resting near an imposing mansion, Carisbrooke House, several shots were fired at them. They thought Carisbrooke

House was occupied by rebel snipers, but when they charged it they found it empty. The shots had actually come from Volunteers who had been there but had taken cover on the grounds and in surrounding fields.

The British pushed on in short advances, lying flat between each movement while scouts reconnoitered ahead. Inside No. 25 Northumberland Road, Mick Malone picked up a pair of field glasses and searched the road toward Carisbrooke House. He saw a big, khaki-clad force advancing with fixed bayonets.

"Give them a volley!" Malone ordered. The rebels' rifles barked, and ten Sherwood Foresters fell.

Lieutenant Colonel Cecil Fane had been given the task of taking the Mount Street Bridge. "Drop!" he ordered the advance party, and the survivors hit the ground.

"Give 'em another!" Malone yelled. This time the volley revealed the rebels' position in No. 25. "That house there!" Fane shouted. "Prepare to fire!"

The British fired a volley, and Fane then ordered a charge.

Their rush on the house might have been successful if Section-Commander Reynolds in Clanwilliam House had not seen what was up. He had his men give the British attackers of No. 25 a fusillade that felled seven and scattered the rest.

Fane and his Robin Hoods, caught between the fire from the two houses and that of the rebels who had left Carisbrooke House, were in desperate straits. While concentrating heavy fire on the houses, he ordered a detachment to try and encircle No. 25 to the left. Mick Malone, at its bathroom window, had them right in his deadly sights. He methodically picked off most of the encircling party, and when it continued on it ran into unexpected fire from Clanwilliam

House. The officer in charge of the party and his other officers were shot down and the force driven back. Another detachment, sent to aid the encircling party, was cut to ribbons by Mick Malone's unerring fire.

A solid mass of about sixty Britishers then tried to storm Mount Street Bridge. Fewer than a dozen got past Parochial Hall, close to the bridge and occupied by the rebels, and this attempt too was driven off.

But for an incredible piece of bungling, the British, far superior in numbers, might easily have carried the bridge. The reinforcements had been put aboard a transport in Liverpool with such rash haste that not a single hand grenade, machine gun or piece of artillery went with them. Thus, in spite of the enemy's greater numbers, the Irish had the advantage in their strong, concealed and protected outposts.

When Lieutenant Colonel Fane tried another encircling movement, this time to the right, to no avail, he sent an urgent message to Ballsbridge for hand grenades and machine guns. But without waiting for them he launched another massive attack in which his men were again driven back with sickening, bloody slaughter.

Late that afternoon the heaviest British attack of all began. The soldiers crawled on their bellies toward the bridge, but from Clanwilliam House each man was killed or wounded as he reached the bridge entrance, and the creeping phalanx never got beyond the ever-increasing pile of dead and wounded at the entrance.

Finally, Brigadier General W. H. M. Lowe, in command of all British forces in Dublin, was reached by telephone. "The bridge *can* be taken," he was told, "but there'll be heavy casualties. Is the situation sufficiently serious to demand the taking of this position at all costs?"

"I think it is," replied Lowe.

The supreme effort began. Attack waves came at twenty-foot intervals. Only once did soldiers get across the bridge, but they were in such disorder, with so many wounded, that the rebels held up their fire to let the survivors crawl to safety under the bridge.

In the schools near the bridge, Section-Commander O'Donoghue's men were exhausted from continuous firing and the sun's heat. He sent a message to Boland's Bakery: "When can we expect relief?" The answer was: "There are no reliefs."

Probably de Valera, at Boland's Bakery, expected that the massive British reinforcements would destroy the outposts, and he would need every man of his little force to hold this last obstacle in the path of the British. He was doubtless right in his caution, but if ever defenders needed fresh men to help them, it was those at the outposts. For about five hours of fearfully bloody fighting, a handful of rebels had held off an entire British battalion.

At five that afternoon the British received the bombs and machine guns which they had urgently requested from headquarters. It was the beginning of the end for the Irish outposts, yet Mick Malone and James Grace at No. 25 threw back two of three assaults. Then the front door of the house disappeared in a great blast of flame, as guncotton tied to it by a creeping squad of British was exploded.

Malone, Grace and their few men retreated to the floor above after placing booby traps on the stairs. From there they poured lead into the British who burst in. Neither Irish leader had a thought of surrender. Their position was hopeless, but they would die fighting.

Malone saw that the end was near. "Get down to the ground floor," he ordered Grace. The British who had come in the front door were dead or wounded or had retreated. But as Grace waited for Malone to join him, another British detachment charged through the back door. Grace emptied his revolver at them as he heard Malone shout, "All right, Séamus [Gaelic for James], I'm coming."

Malone didn't make it. Grace heard a volley and knew Mick had given his life for the Republic of Ireland as he came down the stairs. He himself managed to escape with his life along with some others in the darkness that had fallen.

There remained Clanwilliam House. The British plastered it with machine gun fire from the belfry of a neighboring church. As the Sherwood Foresters charged the house, the rebels met them with a torrent of lead, but an exploding grenade made a shell of the ground floor, destroyed most of the stairs and started a jet of water spurting from a ruptured pipe. Then an explosion set the roof afire. At last, with a British assault wave approaching, George Reynolds saw that remaining longer could only sacrifice the lives of his remaining men. "Come on, lads, we can't do any more," he said.

They were his last words. George Reynolds was killed in the retreat, though most of his men escaped over a back wall. Another heroic fighter was lost to Ireland. As for Clanwilliam House, and the one next to it, both were gigantic flaming torches.

Close by, in Boland's Bakery and at the surrounding outposts, there was panic as de Valera's men waited for the inevitable attack. The exhausted Robin Hoods had been relieved by South Staffordshire troops—also inexperienced but tough young men from the Midland industrial and coal-mining area of England, the Black Country. They might easily have overwhelmed de Valera's frazzle-nerved men in an early-morning assault, but it did not come. Meanwhile, the men from the outposts had been recalled to the bakery. It was noon before the *Helga*'s naval gun, taken off the ship and mounted within range of the bakery, began to bombard it.

De Valera was in wretched condition, having had little if any sleep for two days. He had taken off his puttees and went among his men to encourage them—a tall, gaunt, melancholy figure in bright-red socks. Yet he surmounted his exhaustion and, whatever his lack of military ability, his agile mind produced a plan to save Boland's Bakery.

"Bring me a green flag," he ordered. Then, to Captain Michael Collins: "Take three men and occupy the distillery tower."

The tower loomed high over all else in the area. At the sight of the green flag fluttering from its roof, the *Helga*'s gun boomed. The British thought a dangerous force of rebels was in the tower. Twice the shell missed, but the third made a direct hit, bursting a big water tank and nearly drowning Collins and his men.

Then, without explanation, but doubtless with the thought that the rebel force in the tower had been put out of action, the bombardment ended. De Valera's ruse had accomplished its purpose temporarily, though he was sure that artillery might blast the bakery at any moment.

But the attack never came. News of the rebel surrender did not reach Boland's Bakery until the following day, Sunday, April 30. De Valera and his vice-commandant had been discussing a plan to escape to the Dublin Mountains and carry on the fight from there if necessary. When de Valera saw the surrender order, he did not believe it, and his men favored staying on and continuing their resistance. But at last the commandant was convinced, and his men were made to see that they had to obey the order from Pearce. All slogged to British headquarters in Ballsbridge, where de Valera officially surrendered.

When some five thousand British troops had fought and filtered their way past the rebel outposts into central Dublin, General Lowe decided to stamp out the rebellion by throwing a cordon around the heart of the city. The line of troops would run from the Kingsbridge railway station on the western fringe of the city eastward, just south of the Liffey, to Dublin Castle and on to Trinity College. When more reinforcements arrived, including four huge eighteen-pounder cannon, Lowe set out to establish a second line joined to the first, running through the northern suburbs.

By driving wedges into the rebel positions, the British could gradually draw this steel line tighter and tighter like the drawstring of some gigantic bag. Eventually all the rebel positions inside it, including the Four Courts and General Post Office, would be caught in the trap and squeezed out of existence.

The plan was a good one. So far the rebel outposts had been unable to keep reinforcements from streaming into Dublin. Even the Sherwood Foresters, who had suffered such slaughter around Mount Street Bridge, did not have to attack Boland's Bakery because they had now taken the more inland route used by the other half of the British reinforcements from Kingstown. All went well until they ran into big trouble near the South Dublin Union.

Commandant Kent and his men, holed up in the Nurses' Home, had lost touch with their main outposts at Jameson's

Distillery and Roe's Malt House, as well as General Headquarters, but the men at the outposts were nevertheless ready
to fight to the end.

A force of the Robin Hoods entered the Union grounds,
was fired on and saw a Sinn Fein flag flying from the Nurses'
Home. The invaders knew it was occupied when a report, a
flash and a puff of smoke came from a window.

Forty Britishers advanced in short rushes across five or six
hundred feet of open space under murderous rebel fire, and
were finally forced to take cover in one of the Union buildings, where they met a second British party. They went
through some hospital wards, but the Nurses' Home windows
were so well barricaded that no riflemen were posted at windows overlooking it. The ranking captain of the troops led
a platoon in a dash to a line of low buildings connected to
the Nurses' Home. They advanced through them and finally
knocked a hole through a wall into a heavily barricaded
room, dark and full of dust.

Beyond this room was the lobby of the Nurses' Home. A
wide, heavily barricaded archway divided it, and from this
barrier protruded rifle muzzles. The British captain lobbed
a grenade over the barrier, and its explosion scattered the
Irish behind it.

Commandant Kent knew that the fight was hopeless. He
ordered the Nurses' Home evacuated. But tigerish little
Cathal Brugha, wounded by grenade fragments and then by
a bullet, collapsed there and refused to be moved as his companions left, remaining to blast away at the British.

Those who left had huddled outside, expecting only death.
Suddenly they heard someone inside the Nurses' Home singing, "God save Ireland." It was Brugha, at the barricade.

Whenever he stopped singing, he would hurl a challenge at the British to come out and fight. The others were so inspired that they went back to the barricade, and their fire was so fierce that the British assault party was diven off.

General Lowe had completed his cordon. The rebels at the South Dublin Union, Jameson's Distillery, Jacob's Biscuit Factory, the College of Surgeons and Boland's Bakery were cut off from communication with the General Post Office. But strong rebel outposts in the northern part of the city still held a way open for a retreat to Northern Ireland.

Rebels behind a barricade there were exposed to machine gun fire from the Broadstone railway station, as well as from a great eighteen-pounder nearby. The shells from the big gun demolished most of the barricade, driving its occupants back to a second one farther south, but this too was soon carried away by shrapnel. The rebels finally fled in disorder, and by nightfall the Irish defenses in the north were gone.

General Lowe still had the Four Courts and the College of Surgeons to deal with. In the Four Courts and its outposts, Commandant Daly's Volunteers felt the pressure as the British cordon tightened. All of Church Street, alongside the Four Courts, was under sniper fire from just across the Liffey. One of these expert British snipers picked off thirty-five rebels before he himself was killed.

The Lancers who had unwittingly blundered into the first action of the uprising were able to make things hot for the Volunteers in and around the Four Courts from their refuge in the nearby Medical Mission, since they had the arms and ammunition they had been escorting. The Volunteers tried to set the building afire with a flaming arrow tied with rags soaked in gasoline, but the Lancers put it out.

On Friday morning, April 28, the Robin Hoods moved out of Dublin Castle for an assault on the Four Courts. The leading column got across the Liffey even though the bridge there was swept by fire, and began erecting barricades around the Four Courts. Meanwhile, armored cars that had been brought in dropped men off at the houses in the vicinity armed with crowbars and hatchets. They occupied houses, all the time moving closer to their objective. At the same time, they released the Lancers from their refuge.

The rebels had set the nearby, unoccupied Linenhall Barracks afire. That night a wholesale druggist's shop next to the barracks burst into flame. Inflammables exploded, making the shop a fiery furnace. Blazing barrels of oil shot into the air to explode like rockets with the roar of bursting shells.

General Sir John Maxwell arrived from England that day to take over command in Ireland. He ordered the Four Courts taken by drawing a small cordon around it. This led to the most vicious and continuous fighting of the entire week, since the Irish had the strongest outposts around North King Street, just north of the Four Courts.

The armored cars gave the British a tremendous advantage, for rifle bullets rattled harmlessly off their steel sides as they rolled along, dropping off assault parties at houses along North King Street. It was a fight to the death—the Irish behind their barricades and the tough Staffords sent against them firing from windows and behind chimney pots.

The battle raged most furiously around Reilly's Pub at the corner of Church and North King streets. A barricade opposite commanded a stretch of two hundred yards, and the three

Volunteers in the tower of Jameson's Malt House had command of the whole area. One of them picked off a Britisher every time he saw a flash of rifle fire from the houses along the street. And now at last the Irish had some grenades to drive off armored cars that approached too close to the barricades. When the British tried to lob grenades onto the barriers from rooftops the bombs missed and the throwers were driven off by a storm of rifle fire.

Night fell, but the rifle fire continued. At the barricade outside Reilly's Pub, the Volunteers sang as the Staffords poured volley after volley into the pub without effect, and gave the enemy a furious baptism of lead.

The commander of the Staffords then lost his head and did a foolish thing. His men had advanced only two hundred yards in twelve hours, but now he sent four platoons charging in on the barricades with bayonets fixed. Seven riflemen in Reilly's Pub stopped the charge with a terrific fusillade of lead. The British officer in command was wounded, his troops scattered and many were slaughtered. Yet it was plain that if the Staffords had been kept at tunneling through the houses and creeping up on the barricades from the rear, the Irish would have had no chance.

As it was, however, British might was beginning to tell. Through the night in Reilly's, the men plastered the street with fire, taking turns as barrels grew too hot to allow rifles to be fired. But their ammunition was running low, and the pub was under constant rifle and machine gun fire from front and rear. A man sent out in a desperate attempt to get more ammunition was shot dead. By dawn the Volunteers' situation was hopeless. They managed to escape safely, leaving the pub to the victorious Staffords, who had paid such a high price for it. Yet Commandant Daly and his men still held the Four Courts.

In the College of Surgeons across from St. Stephen's Green, Michael Mallin had a daring plan to drive the British out of the United Services Club. If it succeeded, the houses on the north side of the Green, the club and perhaps the Shelbourne itself would go up in flames. A force was to tunnel through to the corner of Grafton Street and the Green's northern edge, dash across the street in the darkness and set fire to the corner house. The flames would then spread along the street. But at the last minute the plan was abandoned as suicidal.

Mallin's force no longer had information from the General Post Office about the progress of the rising, but his spirits and those of Countess Markievicz and their men and women were good. Their food supply ran perilously low, but they managed to find some rice in the College of Surgeons to tide them over.

Their greatest difficulty came from snipers in buildings on the north side of the Green. It took the Irish a while to discover that a female figure visible in a window of the Shelbourne was a British sniper dressed as a maid. "She" was then shot through the head.

In spite of privation and danger, Countess Markievicz remained gay and confident. She simply did not know the meaning of fear. Michael Mallin's men still held the College of Surgeons when the surrender order came on Saturday, April 29. The countess marched proudly beside Mallin and surrendered to the British captain who had come to receive the capitulation. He accepted her great Mauser rifle-pistol and said, "I can place a motorcar at your disposal, madam."

"No," she replied with great dignity, "I shall march at the head of my men, as I am second in command and shall share their fate."

And thus ended another episode of heroism and hopeless defense by the Irish rebels.

Chapter 6

SACKVILLE STREET
and SURRENDER

THE REBELS from the General Post Office systematically forti-
fied the opposite side of Sackville Street from the Nelson
Pillar to O'Connell Bridge, and stretched wire in front of
the Post Office to keep back the crowds that persisted in gathering there. North of the Pillar, looters had a field day. They
took everything they could lay their hands on. "Shawlies,"
with no idea of the value of what they had taken from jewelry
shops, offered to sell diamond rings and gold watches for a
shilling. The mob watched in delight as a burning store's
stock of fireworks went up in a spectacular display.

General Lowe set up another small cordon like the one
around the Four Courts. This one enclosed the General Post
Office from south of the Liffey in a wide, very rough circle.
On Wednesday afternoon, British troops occupied buildings
along Aston's Quay, running westward from O'Connell
Bridge along the south bank of the river, taking posts at windows and on roofs. And a machine gun was mounted just
south of the bridge, commanding Sackville Street.

As this gun began firing, two nine-pounder cannon on
Trinity College roof also opened fire. The shock of the ex-

73

plosions broke every window in the vicinity of the college and even shook the walls of the General Post Office. Machine guns on top of the Custom House, the Tivoli Theatre and other buildings joined the bombardment.

Brennan Whitmore, in command of a strong rebel barricade in Sackville Street, and his men tunneled through to the Imperial Hotel on the east side. From its windows his riflemen replied as best they could to the British storm of fire.

In spite of rumors flying about the General Post Office that a British assault was coming, Padraic Pearse was calm and confident. His men, however, were fearful. On the roof a white-haired priest, stooping low, gave the rebels in that perilous position absolution.

Suddenly, a strange vehicle lumbered into view on Sackville Street. It was the first of the armored cars built by the British. They had obtained two big iron steam boilers, put holes and slits in the sides and mounted them on motor trucks. Eighteen soldiers could be jammed into each.

Volunteers at a barricade up Sackville Street gazed helplessly at this queer monster. Plainly, bullets could do nothing against it. But one rebel, a crack shot, evidently scored a direct hit on a vital spot of the car. The unwieldy giant stopped and remained there. But these homemade imitations of the new and powerful weapon being used on the Western Front in Europe, the tank, gave the British a strong advantage.

Padraic Pearse sat most of the time on a high stool near the front entrance of the General Post Office. Other leaders sat on upturned barrels there on the ground floor discussing strategy. Nearby were mattresses on which they slept. James Connolly bustled about everywhere, seeing that defenses were strengthened and the men kept busy at new tasks. He had ordered barricades erected on the north side of the building to protect an escape route if it became necessary.

Since it was too dangerous to send messengers back and forth across Sackville Street between the Imperial Hotel and the Post Office, Brennan Whitmore tied quarter-pound weights to lengths of cord and flung the weights across. On the third try one came close enough so that someone in the Post Office could dash out and seize it. Over this line, so slender as to be almost impossible to sever with rifle fire, messages traveled back and forth, high up.

Owing to a misunderstanding of orders, the rebels in the Dublin Bread Company on the east side of Sackville Street had abandoned the building. This soon caused every other building on that side to be deserted. James Connolly's taut nerves snapped when he learned of it.

"I want thirteen volunteers to occupy the buildings on lower Sackville Street," he barked. "We've got to make it as costly as possible for the British if they charge across the bridge."

He had his men instantly, including most of those who had been in the buildings before. They crossed the street under fire, but without losses, and made their way southward through the buildings. All went well until they had to cross Lower Abbey Street to reach the Imperial Hotel in such a storm of fire that only eight of the thirteen got there. But in spite of the terrific bombardment of that part of Sackville Street, the remaining volunteers held the British to an advance that would have taken them several weeks to clear the area of rebel resistance.

James Connolly's confidence remained unbounded. Padraic Pearse too was optimistic. He had issued several communiqués saying the country was rising in arms. Actually, two small towns were seized in the west, in Galway, and railway lines to Limerick in the southwest and centrally located Athlone had been cut. In the southeast the rebels had occupied two towns in County Wexford, cut railway lines, blocked roads and cut communications. Otherwise, in the countryside, there were only a few skirmishes with the British. But Pearse could truthfully report that most of his strong points in Dublin were holding their own.

Most people in Dublin detested the whole business. Food was running short, there were no bread or milk deliveries and no work, banks were closed, there were no separation allowances, there was no mail and civilians were being killed by stray bullets. In the slums the poor were in terrible condition, and all over the city food stores were either sold out or being looted.

About ten o'clock on Wednesday, April 26, a field gun sent a shell crashing into the *Irish Times* printing plant on lower Sackville Street. Huge rolls of newsprint were set afire. The flames then spread to a large rebel barricade on Lower Abbey Street, and they jumped across to Wynn's Hotel, which had become a sort of grandstand for spectators at its windows. Then, when the fire veered up Sackville Street, the British worked their way into the broad thoroughfare, but they got only to Abbey Street, where rebel fire stopped them.

By early afternoon, although all of Lower Abbey Street was being rapidly consumed, the flames crept more slowly up lower Sackville Street, but great billows of smoke and flame obscured all of it.

In the General Post Office, James Connolly, who never gave a thought to his own safety, was getting ready for the last stand against the British. He strode outside and up Henry Street, where he placed detachments in buildings there. Then he went into Princes Street on the south side of the Post Office to oversee the building of a big barricade. A bullet ripped into his right arm, but he paid no attention. Back in the Post Office, he had the flesh wound dressed, forbidding the hospital people to mention it.

That afternoon another armored car came down Henry Street. This time it was stopped when someone tossed a bomb at it. But at about three o'clock a British shrapnel shell shattered the Post Office roof, wounding several men. Pearse ordered the rest down.

Pearse and Connolly decided that the brave women who had stayed in the building, giving untold comfort and relief to the men, would have to leave. Some flatly refused and were allowed to stay.

Mouths must have fallen open in the General Post Office when Connolly put John McLoughlin in charge of thirty men to carry out a dangerous, important mission. John was fifteen years old. But Connolly knew his men. McLoughlin was a tall, strong boy who spoke sensibly, had ideas and was energetic and persistent.

Connolly thought the British would assault Sackville Street from Lower Abbey Street on the east side and Middle Abbey Street on the west. McLoughlin and his men were to occupy the *Irish Independent* office in Middle Abbey Street to stop the British coming in from there.

Connolly himself led McLoughlin's party through an alley to Middle Abbey Street. He waited until they had dashed across to the newspaper office safely. He stayed just too long. A British bullet struck the pavement and ricocheted with a screech, hitting Connolly's ankle. He fell, contorted with pain, but began to drag himself, every inch an agony, back through the alley. He crawled 110 yards before he collapsed in the gutter. His men in the General Post Office then saw him and carried him inside, bleeding very badly.

A British medical officer who was a prisoner treated Connolly even though he was not obligated to do so. The leg bone was smashed just above the ankle, with the ends of the bone sticking through the flesh. He was in excruciating pain.

They stopped the bleeding with a tourniquet and managed to get some chloroform to give Connolly blessed unconsciousness while the British medical man fished out bits of broken bone, tied off ruptured blood vessels and gave Connolly an injection of pain-killing morphine.

When Connolly was conscious, he called the medical officer to his bedside. He managed a grin as he said, "You know, you're the best thing we've captured this week!" Yet he suffered terrible pain in spite of the morphine.

For a long time the Dublin Bread Company remained undestroyed while other buildings around it burned or were blasted to rubble. At ten that night an oil works opposite the Post Office burst into flames. Fire shot several hundred feet into the air, and many oil drums exploded with a terrifying roar. In the Post Office the flooring, windows and barricades had to be drenched from hoses time after time, and often the water turned to steam.

Meanwhile, the British cordon was closing tighter. All through the night rifle and machine gun fire continued. Sackville Street was becoming an inferno.

Brennan Whitmore and his men in the Imperial were now in danger of being incinerated. They shouted across to the Post Office and were told to come over if they could. Four of the men dashed across safely, but under such heavy fire that Whitmore and the rest slipped into a back alley, hoping to circle to the north and make it that way. They got out just in time. The whole front of the Imperial and the building next to it collapsed in a holocaust of flame.

Both Whitmore and a young man who was to become very famous in the Irish Republic, Séan Lemass, were wounded as they crossed a side street, and their men scattered. But they finally found refuge and got some sleep in a slum tenement jammed with people and infested with fleas.

All around the collapsed Imperial, rebel soldiers were singing *The Soldiers' Song:*

> *Soldiers are we,*
> *Whose lives are pledged to*
> *Ireland!*

In the General Post Office, Padraic Pearse issued a statement praising his men and saying that if they lost the fight they would at least have deserved to win it. He added, "Both Eóin MacNeill and we have acted in the best interests of Ireland. For my part, as to anything I have done in this, I am not afraid to face either the judgment of God or the judgment of posterity."

James Connolly, knowing the struggle was nearly over now, said, "Put me into some kind of a stretcher and take me to the front hall, where I can resume command."

They knew he was in agony, but obeyed. He was lifted onto a small bed and carried in, vastly reviving the spirits of the men there. Connolly issued a statement, far from the truth, but optimistic. It ended, "Again, boys, we are winning."

The British cordon around Sackville Street was slowly drawing even tighter with the aid of barricades, artillery, the stubby, powerful little cannon called mortars and, mainly on the roofs, machine guns. A field gun was set up to command Henry Street and prevent an escape from the Post Office by that route.

A number of British prisoners were locked in a cellar of the building. "You'll escape with your lives, I promise you," The O'Rahilly told them.

A furious bombardment was now concentrated on the east side of Sackville Street below the Post Office. Yet twenty rebels in a shop there still held out.

In the slum tenement refuge, the fleas' savage bites woke Captain Whitmore just as a British detachment burst in. Groggy with sleep, he rashly fired at the officer in charge. When none of Whitmore's force would admit firing the shot, the lieutenant ordered them all lined up and shot, but a British captain appeared just in time to intervene and they were made prisoners instead.

A British incendiary shell set the Post Office roof afire. The rebels hauled up hose lines and put it out. Seconds later another shell started a new fire. The rebels fought it fiercely; when bullets shattered the water pipes below, they passed up water buckets in place of the useless hoses. But it was hopeless. Clouds of choking black smoke filled the Post Office. A whole flaming section of the roof fell in on the firefighters.

A few rebels, led by Father John Flanagan, set out for the nearest hospital, helping carry the sixteen wounded men in the building, along with twelve of the fifteen women, leaving two Red Cross nurses and James Connolly's secretary, Winifred Carney. Connolly refused to leave. "No, my place is with my men," he said. Those who went crawled through tunneled walls to the Coliseum Theatre, where they were forced to take refuge.

Pearse and Connolly decided the General Post Office must be abandoned. Two men tried to find an escape route through the sewers but failed. It was then decided to try to reach a manufacturing company at the head of Sackville Street by dashing through the side door into Henry Street and up Moore Street to the factory. The O'Rahilly volunteered to lead an advance party to the buildings and establish a route for the rest.

By seven that evening the fire in the Post Office was so intense that The O'Rahilly shook hands with each of his volunteers, wished them luck and said, "It will be either a glorious victory or a glorious death, boys." Then he ordered them out through the door on the Henry Street side. Meanwhile, the British prisoners were freed and made a dash for safety westward off Henry Street. Their leader collapsed when he was hit by a machine gun bullet, but was finally rescued by the British. Their only casualty was a Dublin Fusileer, shot dead.

The O'Rahilly's party crept slowly up Henry Street, opening a way through one of the Irish barricades to Moore Street. Then they advanced in two groups, one on each side of the street. As they entered Moore Street, Sherwood Foresters behind a barricade at the head of it opened a stream of fire on them. Some were hit, and others scrambled for cover in doorways. The O'Rahilly was badly wounded, but dragged himself into a lane off Moore Street.

During a lull in the firing, The O'Rahilly struggled to his feet and led the survivors up Moore Street, firing at the British barricade ahead. British sharpshooters picked off more of his men, and he himself was hit again. He propped himself against a wall and scribbled a farewell note to his wife. Then he died. Although he had done all he could to stop the rising, unconditionally, and that Mr. Connolly follows him on a when it went on anyway he fought with great bravery. The O'Rahilly belongs in the front rank of the heroes who gave their lives during the rebellion.

The last of the Post Office garrison left, joined by the men still occupying the Metropole across the street. Young John McLoughlin protested the route chosen to the manufacturing plant. It was on Great Britain Street, which had been in the hands of the British since Thursday. He suggested a route through Henry Street that would lead them to the Four Courts, still rebel-held.

Someone shouted that The O'Rahilly was in trouble in Moore Street. McLoughlin, Michael Collins and most of the garrison darted to the rescue, but British fire blasted them into a disorderly race for cover.

The last to leave were Pearse, Connolly and Miss Carney. They got Connolly onto a stretcher, and what remained of the garrison carried him into Henry Street. Later, Connolly told Nora about it: "There was a young soldier, no more than a boy, alongside me. Whenever there was a burst of fire, he leaned over the stretcher, shielding me with his own body."

Connolly, Plunkett, Clarke, MacDermott and the rest found refuge in a grocery store at the corner of Moore Street and Henry Place. Pearse, bringing up the rear, turned back to the Post Office to make sure no one was left before he joined the others.

The kindly grocer's wife divided a ham she was boiling among the hungry men. Then McLoughlin and MacDermott went outside to supervise building a barricade there, but enemy fire drove them back inside.

Next morning the hospitable grocer's wife gave the rebels breakfast before they began tunneling through the houses in an effort to reach the factory on Great Britain Street. Their progress was made more difficult by the need to get Connolly's stretcher through the holes they bored. Every step of the way was agony for him, since the flesh around his wound had become gangrenous. At last, in a fish shop along Moore Street, they decided to go no farther.

McLoughlin still wanted to try to reach the Four Courts.

"How many men would we lose?" asked Pearse.

"Twenty to thirty in Moore Street. If the British are in strength beyond it, most of us will probably not get through. But we're doomed if we stay here."

Pearse asked, "Will the retreat not involve the loss of civilian life in the populous districts, no matter what route we take?"

"I'm afraid it will," replied McLoughlin.

"Then," said Pearse, "issue orders to cease fire for the next hour." And with that he sent Miss O'Farrell, one of the Red Cross nurses, to ask the British for terms. It was 12:45 P.M. on Saturday, April 29, when she went into the street, carrying a Red Cross flag.

"Come forward!" they shouted to her at the British barricade.

"I demand to see the general," she told them there. They escorted her to the headquarters of Colonel Portal on Great Britain Street. After talking with her, the colonel decided she was a spy, and had her searched for concealed arms and held prisoner. Portal then telephoned General Lowe at Trinity College.

Lowe came at once. He treated Miss O'Farrell like the gentleman he was, but told her, "Go back and tell Mr. Pearse that I will not treat with him at all unless he surrenders stretcher. Unless you are back within half an hour, hostilities will be resumed."

At 2:30 P.M. Padraic Pearse was received by General Lowe on the British side of the barricade at the upper end of Moore Street. Pearse handed Lowe his sword and wrote an order to the commandants of the outposts:

"In order to prevent further slaughter of Dublin citizens, and in the hope of saving the lives of our followers now surrounded and hopelessly outnumbered, the members of the Provisional Government present at Headquarters have agreed to an unconditional surrender, and the Commandants of the various districts in the City and Country will order their commands to lay down their arms."

About nine o'clock that evening the remnant of the General Post Office garrison marched silently from Moore Street up Sackville Street and laid down their arms. As the orders reached the outposts, they too surrendered.

The Easter Week uprising was over. Like all others through the centuries in Ireland, it had been crushed. But, unlike the others, this rebellion was not over. It had only begun.

Chapter 7

THE EXECUTIONS

MORE THAN any other cause of their finally losing Ireland, the executions of rebel leaders carried out by the victorious British were the most important. The first of them, done before the surrender, was actually cold-blooded murder rather than a court-martial's sentence of execution; it was ordered by a British officer who was probably demented.

On Tuesday evening, April 25, Francis Sheehy-Skeffington was making his way homeward in Dublin. He was a gentle, good-natured man, devoted to the cause of Ireland's freedom, but a pacifist strongly opposed to violence in gaining it. He had taken no part in the uprising.

As he approached the Rialto Bridge over the Grand Canal, he saw that it was guarded by British soldiers. To give them no suspicion that he was a rebel sneaking up on them, he walked in the middle of the road and they let him pass. Across the bridge he met an acquaintance who called him by name, and the British officer in charge of the guard recognized it. He sent two soldiers to seize Sheehy-Skeffington.

"Are you in sympathy with the Sinn Feiners?" the lieutenant demanded.

"Yes, but I am not in favor of militarism."

Although the officer saw no reason to hold him, he checked by telephone with headquarters.

"Arrest Sheehy-Skeffington," was the reply.

About midnight, Captain J. C. Bowen-Colthurst arrived and demanded that the prisoner be turned over to him although he had no orders for this.

It would be insulting animals to call Bowen-Colthurst an animal, for he was worse than one. He had Sheehy-Skeffington taken to Portobello Barracks and locked up. The next morning he ordered his prisoner and two others taken from the guardroom into the barracks yard.

"Walk by yourselves to the far wall," he ordered the three men. "Present arms!" he ordered their escort, and then: "Fire!"

A lieutenant who heard the volley came into the yard. He saw Sheehy-Skeffington's legs move and asked what should be done. "Shoot again," commanded Bowen-Colthurst, and a second volley was fired.

Major Sir Francis Vane, outraged by the murder, demanded that an investigation be held. General Maxwell and other officers scoffed at the idea, and one said it was a good thing Sheehy-Skeffington had been put out of the way. In May, Vane went to London and carried the story straight to the famous Lord Kitchener, then Secretary of State for War. Kitchener promised to send a telegram ordering Bowen-Colthurst's arrest.

Vane later claimed that General Maxwell ignored Kitchener's order. At any rate, word of the affair finally reached the attention of Prime Minister Herbert Asquith, who personally went to Ireland to investigate. Bowen-Colthurst was then court-martialed and found guilty, but insane. He was sent to an asylum in England.

As for the rebel leaders, those who had been in the General Post Office and at the outposts were imprisoned, with their men, in Kilmainham Jail and some of the barracks in Dublin. All the leaders except James Connolly were eventually held in Richmond Barracks at the west end of the city.

General Maxwell, a harsh, cold-blooded officer, was determined to make an example of the rebel leaders that would frighten the Irish into strict obedience to British rule. Few greater mistakes were ever made by the British government than to allow him his revenge.

Maxwell wasted no time in trying Padraic Pearse, Thomas MacDonagh and Thomas J. Clarke. Clarke, fifty-eight years old, held no military rank but was recognized as one of the commanders in the General Post Office. Because he was considered the father of the revolution, he had been given the honor of being the first to sign Pearse's Declaration of Independence.

All three were court-martialed on May 3 and taken to Kilmainham Jail after being sentenced to die. None had the slightest chance of escaping the penalty, and this was true of the others who were condemned. Early the next morning the three were marched, one by one, into the gloomy prison yard with its high stone wall, and shot by a firing squad.

The next day, May 4, Edward Daly, Michael O'Hanrahan, Joseph Plunkett and Padraic Pearse's brother William were executed at dawn in the jail. The following day John MacBride was shot.

On May 8 four leaders went to their deaths in Kilmainham

—Séan Heuston, Michael Mallin, Edmund Kent and Con Colbert. Séan Mac Diarmada was court-martialed at Richmond on May 9 and executed on May 12. That same morning James Connolly was shot.

These two were the last of the fourteen Dublin leaders executed. Every one died with dignity, calmness and pride in what he had done for his country. Most saw some members of their families an hour or two before they died. These heart-rending scenes are told in the records of the revolution. Two that are of special interest will be described.

In spite of his serious illness, Joseph Plunkett was engaged to Grace Gifford. But for the rising, expected to begin on Easter Sunday, they would have been married on that day. Plunkett tried desperately, but at first in vain, to arrange a meeting in prison so that they could be married.

Then, miraculously, Grace Gifford was summoned to Kilmainham Jail at 6 P.M. on May 3. For two hours that seemed like a century, she waited there. At eight she was taken to the prison chapel. Then Joseph Plunkett was led in by soldiers with fixed bayonets. The only illumination in the dark chapel was candlelight, and by it the two were married by Father Eugene McCarthy, with two of the soldiers acting as witnesses.

They were separated immediately, but in the early hours of the morning Grace was brought back to Kilmainham. They gave her ten minutes with her husband—ten precious minutes that made it easier for Grace Gifford Plunkett and easier for Joseph Plunkett as he faced the firing squad in the jail yard soon afterward.

As for James Connolly, his eldest daughter (who as this book is written is Mrs. Nora Connolly O'Brien, living in Dublin) has told the story beautifully and touchingly.

After Nora and Agna finished their grueling, perilous walk to Drumconda and were shocked to learn of the surrender and that their father was seriously wounded and under arrest, their first thought was to reach their mother and two younger sisters. They were in Dundrum, a suburb far across Dublin to the south.

The two girls started their dangerous trip the next morning, taking a circuitous route to avoid British barricades, and reached Sackville Street and the O'Connell Bridge. What they saw horrified them—the smoking ruins of central Dublin, dead horses in the streets, crowds of silent people. They were stopped once at a bridge over the Grand Canal by a British guard there, but they cajoled its officer into letting them go on.

Within striking distance of Dundrum they were terror-stricken when they saw a poster from an illustrated English newspaper. It was a picture of their father with the caption: "James Connolly, the dead rebel leader." When the girls finally reached their mother's lodgings, she was weeping uncontrollably, for she too had seen the poster.

"Papa is wounded and a prisoner of war, but that is all," Nora reassured her. "They don't shoot or hang prisoners of war."

The next day Nora found new lodgings in Dublin near Dublin Castle. Once the family had moved in, Agna tried several times in vain at the castle to get permission for her mother to see James Connolly. Their hopes began to sink when they heard of the executions of Sheehy-Skeffington, Pearse, MacDonagh and Clarke.

It seemed an eternity before, on Sunday afternoon, May 8, a note was left in their mailbox: "If Mrs. Connolly will call at Dublin Castle Hospital on Monday or Tuesday after eleven o'clock, she can see her husband."

Mrs. Connolly's joy was shadowed by fear. She was sure this would be her last meeting with him.

When Mrs. Connolly left on Monday, taking the youngest girl, Nora said, "If you get the chance, tell him Agna and I are safe."

"Oh, I'd be afraid to mention your name," her mother cried.

"Well," said Nora, "tell him that Gwendolyn Violet has turned out to be a good walker; that she walked to Dublin." She knew her father would recognize his pet name for her.

Mrs. Connolly and her seven-year-old daughter were thoroughly searched at the castle and made to promise they would give Connolly nothing by which he might take his own life. But they found him so cheerful and apparently so sure he would not be executed that they returned in good spirits.

The next day Nora went with her mother to the hospital. Outside James Connolly's room, Nora saw armed guards with bayonets fixed, and an officer was with the two women in the room. Yet Connolly's cheerfulness made them both feel confident. He said he was not in pain.

"But I have been court-martialed today," he added. "They propped me up in bed. The strain was very great." He said nothing of what he knew: that he was to die.

They had a good talk. Connolly wanted to know everything that had happened when Nora went to Northern Ireland. And with his face aglow he told them about the boy who had shielded him from British bullets in Henry Street.

"We cannot fail now," he said. "Those young lads will never forget."

Near midnight on Thursday, May 11, an ambulance came to the Connollys' lodgings. "James Connolly is very weak and wants to see his wife and eldest daughter," they were told.

The ambulance sped through the dark streets to Dublin Castle. Nora noticed that the vicinity of her father's room was alive with armed guards, and again an officer was stationed inside the room.

"Well, Lillie," James Connolly said to his wife, "I suppose you know what this means?"

"Oh, James! It's not that—it's not that?"

"Yes, Lillie. They waked me at eleven and told me I was to die at dawn." He patted her head. "Don't cry, Lillie, you'll unman me."

"But your beautiful life, James. Your beautiful life."

"Well, Lillie, hasn't it been a full life, and isn't this a good end?"

Nora was weeping. "Don't cry, Nora," he said, "there is nothing to cry about." Then he whispered to her to put her hand under the bedclothes, and he slipped something into it.

"Smuggle that out," Connolly said. "It is my last statement."

He told Mrs. Connolly he wanted her to go with the girls to America, leaving their son Rory, who had fought in the uprising, in Ireland. Nora told her father about the other executions. "All the best men in Ireland are gone," she said.

James Connolly was silent a few moments. Then he said, "I am glad I am going with them."

All too soon the officer in the room said, "You have five minutes more."

They had to give Mrs. Connolly some water. Her husband

tried to take her in his arms, but he could only lift his head and shoulders from the bed.

In no time, it seemed, the officer said, "Time is up."

"Good-by," Connolly said to Nora. "Go to mother."

A nurse helped Mrs. Connolly away. Nora ran back and kissed her father. "Nora, I'm proud of you," he said.

Then they shut the door.

A little before dawn they carried James Connolly on a stretcher to an ambulance and drove to Kilmainham Jail. There they carried him, strapped in a chair, to the jail yard. He was as brave and cool as all the others had been as they set him down against the high wall.

The priest who was with him said, "Will you pray for the men who are about to shoot you?"

"I will pray for all brave men who do their duty," James Connolly replied. And he prayed: "Forgive them, for they know not what they do."

Then the volley rang out.

Nora Connolly waited till after dawn to read her father's statement. It ended proudly:

"I personally thank God that I have lived to see the day when thousands of Irish men and boys, and hundreds of Irish women and girls, were ready to affirm that truth [that the British government had no right in Ireland], and to attest it with their lives if need be."

Of the other important rebel leaders, there remained the Countess Markievicz, Sir Roger Casement and Eamon de Valera. The countess was very angry when they court-martialed and sentenced her to penal servitude for life because she was a woman. Believing that a dead martyr could do more for Ireland than a live rebel, she wanted to die.

As for Sir Roger Casement, after his capture near Tralee, he was taken to the Arbour Hill Detention Barracks in Dublin and then to England, first to Brixton Prison and then to the Tower of London, where for centuries titled Englishmen and royalty accused of high crimes had been imprisoned.

Casement's three-day trial from June 26 to 29 was an international sensation. They tried him not for being a rebel but for treason, since he held a British title. Yet, at Pentonville Prison on August 3, he suffered the humiliation of being hanged like a common criminal.

The only Irish leader in whose case the British showed good sense was Eamon de Valera. He was taken to Richmond Barracks and court-martialed on Monday afternoon, May 8. Like all the other trials, it was short, and he had no chance of escaping a guilty verdict. He was sentenced to be executed and taken to Kilmainham.

Things began to happen swiftly. Already, throughout the civilized world, especially in America, a storm of outrage had arisen over the previous executions. Even in Britain, officials began to doubt the wisdom of it. And de Valera was American-born. Thousands of Irish-Americans, already aroused, would express their wrath publicly if de Valera were shot. And Britain was desperately hoping for American entrance into World War I as her ally; it could easily save her from losing to Germany.

On the very day of his trial, de Valera was reprieved and sentenced to penal servitude for life. They transferred him from Kilmainham to nearby Mountjoy Prison, a much more comfortable jail.

Nevertheless, the executions of the other leaders had caused a tide of indignation that not only won the Irish rebels friends in America, Britain itself and other countries, but unified the Irish nation. Indeed the revolution was far from over. Pearse, Connolly, Plunkett and the other leaders had not died in vain.

Chapter 8

THE BIG FELLOW and THE START of the TROUBLES

MEANWHILE, Dublin was under martial law, her government and daily life completely controlled by the British army. And all over Ireland, police and soldiers were arresting men suspected of being Sinn Feiners—more than all of the Volunteers who took part in the Easter Week uprising. Like the prisoners of the rising, thousands of them were deported to prisons in England and Scotland. Conditions aboard the ships that ferried them across the Irish Sea were terrible, but the captives were heartened by the hoarse cheers of great crowds at the docks as they left Ireland.

This was only the beginning of the solid Irish support for freedom that the men of the Easter rising had not had. All over the country there were public demonstrations against the deportations. And in a letter to General Maxwell, published in Irish newspapers, the Most Reverend Dr. Edward Thomas, Bishop of Limerick, wrote:

"You took care that no plea for mercy should interpose on behalf of the poor young fellows who surrendered to you in Dublin. The first intimation which we got of their fate was the announcement that they had been shot in cold blood.

I regard your action with horror, and I believe that it has outraged the conscience of the country." After condemning the deportation of the prisoners without trial, he concluded, "Altogether, your regime has been one of the worst and blackest in the history of the misgovernment of this country."

When Prime Minister Asquith came to Ireland to investigate the Bowen-Colthurst affair, he became acutely aware of the change that had taken place among the Irish people. In England the famous David Lloyd George had become Secretary of War upon Lord Kitchener's death aboard a British warship sunk by the Germans. Lloyd George who would soon become Prime Minister, was extremely worried about the Irish situation.

Worst of all, feeling against Britain was high in the United States. A powerful New York newspaper denounced the British actions in Ireland. President Woodrow Wilson, in an address May 27, 1916, although he did not mention Ireland by name, said, "We believe these fundamental things: First, that every people has a right to choose the sovereignty under which they shall live. . . . Second, that the small states of the world have a right to enjoy the same respect for their sovereignty and for their territorial integrity that great and powerful nations expect and insist upon."

Lloyd George then proposed that the Home Rule Act of 1914, postponed at that time till the end of the war, be put into effect. Under Home Rule Ireland was to have a Parliament of two houses. The Senate would have 46 members and the House of Commons 164 members, elected by the Irish people. There would be an Irish chief executive.

But Home Rule would be limited to the twenty-six Catholic-dominated counties of southern Ireland. Because the six counties of Northern Ireland, or Ulster, were strongly Protestant and feared they would have no influence in a united Irish government, they were to remain under British rule for at least six years. And Britain reserved a number of important rights she would continue to control in Ireland.

After John Redmond, an influential Irish member of the British Parliament, had explained the plan at a meeting in Dublin, there was a tumult of protest. Redmond, who favored it, then withdrew his support, and for the time being the whole thing was dropped.

Also for the time, the old British-controlled Irish government continued under Lord Wimbourne as Lord Lieutenant. But the country was still at the mercy of the fiercely hated General Maxwell.

Again the uneasy Lloyd George revived the proposed Home Rule for Ireland, and again it failed. When Easter, 1917, came, there was a gigantic demonstration in Dublin, and a declaration that Ireland was a separate nation was drawn up.

Finally, Lloyd George submitted two proposals, of which Ireland might choose either one. The first was that Home Rule should be established in the twenty-six southern counties, but the six of Northern Ireland would be excluded until the British Parliament decided to end it. A governing Council of Ireland would be created in which these six counties would have the same number of representatives as the twenty-six to the south.

The other proposal was that settlement of the question should be discussed by a convention of Irishmen who would submit proposals to the British cabinet for the future government of the country as a part of the British Empire.

Ireland wanted neither plan. The country was bitterly opposed to Partition—the proposed separation of the six counties from the rest of the country. Sir Edward Carson, an influential member of Parliament for the north, persuaded the Ulsterites to accept the idea of a convention; but in the south the Sinn Fein utterly refused to have anything to do with it.

Thus, when the convention began its meetings at Trinity College in Dublin July 25, 1917, it was not unified. Of the proposed 101 members, 15 were selected by the British government and 47 were mayors and other officials under British influence. Only five representatives were allowed Sinn Fein, which ignored the whole thing. The only beneficial result was an agreement under which Britain released the rebel prisoners.

There was little else she could have done, anyway. In the crowded British jails the great horde of prisoners had organized a new Sinn Fein movement. In Ireland their families and friends took it up. The prisoners, many suffering ill treatment and terrible living conditions, chose their own commandants. They disobeyed prison rules and orders from jailers, and in many cases their conditions were improved.

Eamon de Valera was the commandant in famed Dartmoor Prison, standing in the wild, lonely moorlands of Devonshire. His men instantly obeyed any order he issued, and the prison officials were at their wits' end trying to cope with the prisoners' disobedience and unruliness.

Then one day Eóin MacNeill arrived at Dartmoor with other convicted men from Ireland. The prisoners already there had lined up in the gloomy Central Hall for inspection. As MacNeill came down the iron stairs in the center of the hall, de Valera stepped out of ranks and faced his men.

"Irish Volunteers, attention!" he shouted. "Eyes, left!" The salute to MacNeill was given joyously.

De Valera was later shifted to Maidstone Jail and then to Pentonville Prison as a troublemaker, but it didn't stop the prisoners' rebellious actions at Dartmoor. And in most of the jails the situation had got so far out of control that the British government was ready to throw up its hands in despair. The Irish prisoners had won, and after the convention in Dublin they were released.

The first shipload of them, which included de Valera and MacNeill, arrived in Dublin to a tumultuous welcome. That evening, when another ship arrived, the Countess Markievicz was among those aboard. She rode through the streets in a vast, cheering procession. All over Ireland that night huge bonfires blazed on the hills.

Just as de Valera was leaving Pentonville, he had been handed a telegram. He had been chosen to represent the Sinn Fein Party in the election of a member of Parliament from East Clare.

The night after the first prisoners arrived, a group of them who were officers in the Volunteers drew up a message to the President and Congress of the United States, signed by de Valera, MacNeill and twenty-four others. It quoted a statement by President Wilson in which he had said, "No people must be forced under a sovereignty under which it does not wish to live." They expressed the hope that ways would be found to achieve Ireland's goals.

Meanwhile, Irish rebel influence in the British Parliament was growing. Count George Plunkett, father of the executed Joseph, had been elected to it. When the East Clare election was held, de Valera was swept into office after campaigning for no settlement with Britain short of a free Irish Republic. Another Sinn Fein member was elected from Kilkenny.

Demonstrations for a free republic continued all over Ireland. A good many demonstrators were arrested, fined and imprisoned. De Valera, now the chief leader of Sinn Fein, was urging all patriotic Irishmen to wear the Volunteer uniform. Meanwhile, another prominent Sinn Feiner was elected to Parliament.

And in Ireland a new star was rising over the horizon to give Irishmen new hope for freedom—Michael Collins, the same young man who had been Joseph Plunkett's aide in the General Post Office.

Michael Collins was a strange bag of contradictions. He could be ruthless, even savage, ordering the killings of enemies without flickering an eyelash. Yet he could be gentle and was always with old people and children, and he was generous to a fault. He could be tactless, but he learned to be an able negotiator. He could curse so that the air fairly smoked, but when it suited his purposes he was the perfect, charming gentleman. He was tough as an oak knot, yet he loved a good joke and his laughter was infectious. And sometimes he wept like a small child.

Perhaps better than anything else, Michael Collins loved a fight—no boxing matches fought by the rules, but rough-and-tumble, battering, hammering brawls in which rules were thrown to the winds, and the dirtier the tactics the better. Collins got into many such dogfights in pubs, for he loved to drink, though he was never a drunkard, and sometimes he would start one elsewhere just because he felt like it.

Collins usually won. He was tall, magnificently built and as strong as a brick wall; he had tremendous energy and knew how to handle his fists—and his feet and legs if necessary.

Look at Michael Collins when he was in prison in England after the Easter Week uprising. One sees a powerful young fellow in his middle twenties, striding about, always busy at something, and with energy that makes him like a steam boiler safety valve about to pop off. He has a wide, good-humored face, brown hair and deep-set, wide-spaced gray eyes, a long, distinguished nose, firm mouth and a bit of a swagger in his walk.

Collins was a natural leader, and he knew how to mix just the right amount of bullying and joking to gain the respect and liking of the British soldiers in the jails where he was confined. The other prisoners worshiped him, and he was the best of inmates. It is not easy in jail to keep clean and neat all the time, but Collins did it. He always had some project to keep him occupied, especially to gain more rights for all the prisoners.

They were not allowed to communicate with each other at first, but Collins managed to do so. When, later on, the prisoners were allowed to fraternize, he was their leader, the beginning of the leadership he was to show later. It was the same when he was transferred from Stafford Jail to the big Frongoch Internment Camp in Wales, crowded with Irish prisoners shifted there from all over England.

"Collins thinks he's a big fellow," the prisoners said admiringly. The name stuck. Michael Collins would go down in Irish history better known as the Big Fellow than by his real name.

When Collins returned to Dublin with the released prisoners, young men of the Volunteers and the secret Irish Republican Brotherhood were gaining control of organizations that could be useful to them. The National Aid Association, which was collecting funds to relieve victims of the rising, was one. The Big Fellow was appointed its secretary. His boundless energy enabled him to work long hours, and the job brought him into contact with many Irish patriot leaders. He was on his way up.

Several organizations were working for the freedom movement, but they did not always agree. Of the two most powerful ones, Sinn Fein demanded complete independence, while the Irish Republican Brotherhood wanted independence but a continued alliance with Britain. It was a good sign when the I.R.B., as it was called, cooperated with Sinn Fein at the latter's annual convention in Dublin.

About 1,700 delegates were present. Arthur Griffith, who had founded Sinn Fein in 1905, addressed them, saying an Assembly was needed to speak for the nation. Cathal Brugha proposed that a new constitution be drawn up, and this was accepted unanimously. Eamon de Valera was elected president of the united organization, which kept the title of Sinn Fein.

In London, Prime Minister Lloyd George watched what was going on with increased anxiety. On October 23, 1917, in the House of Commons, he spoke of de Valera's speeches ". . . to stir people up to rebellion against the authorities."

He added: "There is a great deal of talk among the Sinn Feiners which does not mean Home Rule. . . . It means complete separation. . . . It means secession. The words which are used are 'sovereign independence.' This country could not possibly accept that under any conditions."

A breaking point was coming. World War I provided it. True, the United States had entered the war, but large American forces could not be in Europe for some time. And Russia had deserted the Allies and withdrawn from the war. More soldiers were desperately needed on the Western Front in France, and quickly.

In spite of the many Irish volunteers fighting there, Lloyd George felt that more must be obtained. Members of the British government were urging him to impose conscription— the drafting of Irishmen to fight.

President Wilson was doing all he could to put big American armies in the field as soon as possible, but at the same time he warned Britain that imposing conscription upon Ireland might cause trouble among the great mass of Irish-Americans in the United States.

Nevertheless, on April 8, 1918, a bill was introduced into the British House of Commons under which Irishmen could be drafted whenever the King signed an Order in Council to that effect.

This was the breaking point. It was the origin of what are referred to in Ireland as The Troubles—bitter, ruthless, armed rebellion, beginning against the threat of conscription.

A conference on the subject, held in Dublin, was attended by representatives of the various Irish political parties. De Valera drew up a strong pledge against conscription. It was circulated throughout Ireland and signed by many thousands. To emphasize the protest, the Irish labor unions held a one-day general strike on April 23, 1918, that paralyzed everything all over Ireland except in Belfast.

Britain retaliated by putting Ireland under the military command of Field Marshal Lord French, who replaced Wimbourne as Lord Lieutenant and General Governor. The British government followed this up by announcing that it had discovered a "German plot" in which Irish rebel leaders were implicated. Not a shred of truth was ever proved of it, but it resulted in the arrest of suspected Irish "plotters."

Seventy-three prisoners were deported to England, including de Valera, Arthur Griffith, Count Plunkett and the Countess Markievicz. Michael Collins had learned of the British plan and warned the leaders, but they decided against attempting to escape.

As for the Big Fellow, he made up his mind not to be taken. He reasoned that if he hid in the house of someone who had already been arrested, the police would not come there—and he was right.

When the arrests did not stop the people's rebellious spirit, the police were ordered to help the troops stop night drills the Irish were holding, and close the halls used for them. They were also ordered to seize the flood of literature being distributed urging disobedience to British rule, and the printing presses turning it out. A reward of £500 was offered for information about the landing of arms and ammunition for the rebels. On July 5, 1918, meetings and public processions were forbidden, but they continued. In September, 1918, ninety-six, and in October seventy-one Sinn Feiners who had been rounded up were sentenced to prison.

On October 15 the Order in Council for conscription was signed. The more than 100,000 Volunteers in Ireland who were now organized into an army of sorts considered this a declaration of war. Actually, the order was meaningless, for the armistice signed on November 11, 1918, ended World War I as a victory for the Allies.

Nevertheless, the damage was already done. Ireland was well united and rapidly organizing for another struggle for freedom.

The first move was made following an election of members to a new British Parliament on December 14, 1918. Even though a hundred of its leaders were in jail, Sinn Fein put up candidates from every election district in southern Ireland except two. The result was an overwhelming victory. Of the 105 members of Parliament elected from Ireland, 73 were Republicans, the party to which Sinn Fein was dedicated.

That decided the Republicans to set up a separate Irish government. Dáil Éireann (pronounced "Dawl Eyeran") was convened as an independent governing body of the Irish nation. It met for the first time in Dublin January 21, 1919, and issued a new Declaration of Independence that affirmed the one Padraic Pearse had drawn up in 1916.

The British government was not going to accept all this calmly. Britain was free of her desperate struggle with Germany. She could now give more attention to subduing Ireland once more and continuing the rule she had forced upon the little country for seven and a half centuries.

On the other hand, Britain was facing an almost fully united Ireland instead of the few hundred rebels who had fought British troops almost to a standstill for nearly a week. She was sick of war. There was world opinion to be considered too, especially that in the United States. And in an armed struggle Ireland was going to have the military leadership of a powerful, fearless, skilled, dangerous man—the Big Fellow.

Chapter 9

THE BIG FELLOW
GOES INTO ACTION

IRELAND WANTED to send representatives to the Peace Conference to gain her rights as an independent nation. British influence proved too strong, however, in spite of a resolution passed by the United States Congress supporting Ireland's claim, and Irish participation was denied.

The leaders who were still at liberty in Ireland were a mixed lot in their political beliefs about how an Irish government should be organized and what its relations should be with Britain. For example, Arthur Griffith was one of the moderates. He believed Ireland should be satisfied to have self-government but continue a close connection with Britain. Michael Collins, on the other hand, was the volcano who wanted to plunge into a fight with Britain if Ireland was not given full independence.

Thus, Eamon de Valera's great skill at negotiation, diplomacy and government were badly needed to bring out unity among the Irish organizations, and to negotiate with Britain. But de Valera was in Lincoln Prison in England.

De Valera had been seized by the police before the end of the war when he arrived at Bray Head en route to Greystones, his house on the coast a little to the south of Dublin. They had searched him, but for some unknown reason let him keep his walking stick, which, when unsheathed, became a sword.

On a ridiculous pretext they tried to say he was in contact with a German submarine off the coast there. Then they took him to England aboard a warship. He was first held in jail at Gloucester and then transferred to Lincoln.

De Valera and the other Irish prisoners there were treated well. He was allowed to play handball, one of his favorite sports, with his companions. He was able to obtain books to continue his studies as a professor of mathematics, and a typewriter on which he practiced. The machine was of an unusual design, and he found he could change the alignment of the letters so that they might be used as a code in correspondence. He was also allowed to read the English newspapers.

These concessions did not change de Valera's attitude toward his captors, however. When one of his fellow prisoners fell ill, de Valera went to the prison's governor and told him that there would be trouble if anything happened to the sick man. As a result, he was finally able to get the man released and sent home to Ireland.

In Ireland, meanwhile, more than six months after de Valera had been deported, someone among the Irish leaders suggested that his escape from Lincoln might be accomplished. Michael Collins seized on the idea with feverish zeal. This was the sort of thing he loved—dangerous intrigue and bold strikes for the cause.

The leaders managed to communicate the scheme to de Valera. Since he was such a devoted Catholic, he was a server at all Masses in the prison chapel. During the services he noticed something that made his heart beat a little faster. The chaplain never carried his key to the prison gates with him to the altar, but left it in the sacristy, the room where the vestments and vessels used in the Mass were kept.

De Valera decided to try to get a wax impression of the key, using the stubs of burned altar candles that were left in a drawer in the sacristy. He took some and warmed them until they were soft enough to pack into an empty tobacco tin. He did this just before a Mass at which he got one of his companions to take his place as principal server. He had deliberately neglected to place one of the cruets used in the service on the altar table, and the priest allowed him to go to the sacristy for it.

De Valera darted into the room with the concealed tobacco tin. But to his intense disappointment the wax was too hard to get an impression of the key. So he put the tin next to his skin, where the wax would be warmed, and before the Mass was over used another pretext to go back to the sacristy. This time he got the wax impression. Later, with the greatest care, he cut pieces of paper into the exact shape of the impression; from these a duplicate key could be made.

Then began a long, complex, dangerous and frustrating process of sending the paper to Ireland and getting back a key to the gates. His idea of how to send it was fiendishly clever. Among the prisoners was a man who was something of an artist. Since it was December, de Valera got this man to draw a most unusual Christmas card.

It showed Séan McGarry, one of the prisoners, a little tipsy and trying to put a large key in a small keyhole. Under it was written, "Xmas, 1917, can't get in." Below it was another picture of McGarry looking at the keyhole of his cell door with the inscription, "Xmas, 1918, can't get out."

Inside the card, one of the prisoners wrote a note:
"My dear Tommie,

"The best wishes I can send are those that de Valera wrote
in my autograph book. Field will translate."

"Field" was a code name that Michael Collins used. There
followed a note written in Gaelic by de Valera, explaining
that the key in the picture was an exact drawing of the jail
key, and the keyhole was a cross-section of it. De Valera
asked that a duplicate key be sent in a cake, along with some
files, and that when he made his escape attempt he be met
outside the prison.

His Irish rescuers could set the date by sending Séan Mc-
Garry a letter saying, "Billie got up the —th [filling in the
date] of last month. Is now quite well."

Prisoners' mail is usually censored, but if the Christmas
card was, the prison authorities must have seen nothing
wrong with this rather queer Christmas greeting to Mrs.
McGarry, for they evidently let it through without trying to
translate the Gaelic.

As the poet Robert Burns wrote, "The best laid schemes
o' mice and men . . ." often go wrong. Mrs. McGarry seems
to have received the card, all right, but thought it was just
a joke. At any rate, it did not reach the Sinn Fein leaders.

One can imagine de Valera's anxiety and fears when no
package or message came to Lincoln. So he got one of the
prisoners to write a friend of his, an Irish Catholic curate in
Leeds, England, an appeal, written in Latin, to send the
letter to Mrs. McGarry. It contained, among other incon-
sequential things, details about the prison and a possible
escape route.

No reply to either communication had been received by
January 10, 1919. Another letter was written containing a

paragraph or two in de Valera's handwriting, as proof that this was not a British ruse. This time it and the paper copy of the key impression reached the Irish leaders.

The cake finally arrived at Lincoln Prison. Jailers are always suspicious of such gifts, and the chief warder prodded it with a knife while de Valera held his breath. Fortunately, the knife struck nothing hard. Inside the cake were the duplicate key and the files—but, alas, the key was defective and would not turn the locks.

Twice more cakes were sent, and each time the unfortunate de Valera found the keys in them defective. Finally a fourth arrived with one that fitted perfectly. The date for the escape had to be sometime about February 3, while the moon was only a crescent and its light dim. A signal was to be made by the rescuers when they reached the prison. The escape had to be made before the cell doors were locked for the night, since they could not be unlocked from the inside. About 7 P.M. would be ideal, giving the three prisoners who planned to escape—de Valera, Séan McGarry and Séan McElroy—at least two hours before they were likely to be missed.

With the Big Fellow on the rescue mission was his friend Harry Boland. They crossed to Manchester, England, where a friend hid them. When the time was right for the escape, Collins and Boland drove to the proper place outside Lincoln Prison early in the evening of February 3. The Big Fellow had checked and rechecked every detail to make sure nothing would go wrong. He had even tested the rope ladder they brought with them.

The Big Fellow snapped on a flashlight. Inside, at his cell window, de Valera struck three or four matches in a bundle as an answering signal. For a time that seemed an hour to the agitated de Valera, Collins' flashlight continued to shine; the catch on it was stuck. While Collins wrestled with it, uttering curses that were soft but smoking, Boland seized the flashlight and put it out of sight in his pocket.

It was about 7:40 P.M. As quietly as possible the three prisoners made their way along, unlocking doors as they went. What they thought was the last barrier, the back gate, opened easily too, but they found still another in the wall. De Valera pushed his key into the lock. To his horror, it broke off.

The rescuers were just outside. Harry Boland had a duplicate key. When de Valera, in low tones, told him what had happened, Boland carefully pushed his key into the lock from the other side while de Valera uttered a silent prayer. To the relief of all, the broken-off piece was pushed out and fell to the ground.

Boland's key opened the lock. The gate, rusty because it was seldom used, made a creak like the door of a haunted house that to the prisoners sounded like a siren. They left it open rather than risk having someone in the prison hear it close.

The prisoners drove to Manchester and safe hiding. It was 9:30 P.M. before the escape was discovered in Lincoln Prison. By the following day the Irish newspapers had the story, to the immense delight of the Irish people.

For some time de Valera's whereabouts were unknown. He stayed hidden in Manchester for a couple of weeks. During that time Cathal Brugha arrived from Ireland and conferred with him. Brugha and some of the other leaders, including the reckless Big Fellow, had a plan to retaliate against the British government for imprisoning rebels without trial by assassinating its cabinet members, but de Valera, as President of the newly organized nation, would not approve it.

By February 18, arrangements had been made for him to

go to Liverpool, board a ship and sail for Dublin. He was secretly smuggled aboard the vessel and arrived in Dublin on February 20. Since he was still in danger of being rearrested, he was secreted in a college on the north side of the city. There he held conferences with the leaders of the Dáil Éireann. They were still hoping—in vain—that Ireland's freedom would be obtained at the Peace Conference.

Actually, de Valera's escape was meaningless. Once again Britain was finding its Irish prisoners too hot to handle. On March 6 the House of Commons voted to release them.

Since there appeared to be no hope of freedom for Ireland at the Peace Conference, de Valera decided to go to the United States and appeal directly to the American people. He left Dublin on June 1, 1919, for Liverpool. In England he was still in danger of arrest for his jail break, so he was smuggled aboard a steamer and made the crossing to America.

In the meantime, the Big Fellow, itching for new action, decided to get Robert Barton, a former British officer converted to the Irish cause, out of jail in Dublin, where the British had imprisoned him. Collins and some of his Volunteers managed to arrange a plan of escape with Barton.

On a quiet Sunday evening, Collins and his men gathered outside the jail. Barton had sawn through a bar in his cell with files smuggled to him, and had fashioned a dummy to leave in his cell to fool inspecting jailers.

Barton saw his rescuers and signaled to them, then got through his cell window. Collins and his men threw a rope ladder over the wall. Barton climbed it, jumped down into a blanket held by those outside and was spirited away to safe hiding.

An even more valuable prisoner to the Big Fellow was Padraic Fleming. Fleming was a real firebrand who had been

Irish Provinces and Counties

POBLACHT NA H EIREANN.

THE PROVISIONAL GOVERNMENT
OF THE
IRISH REPUBLIC
TO THE PEOPLE OF IRELAND.

IRISHMEN AND IRISHWOMEN: In the name of God and of the dead generations from which she receives her old tradition of nationhood, Ireland, through us, summons her children to her flag and strikes for her freedom.

Having organised and trained her manhood through her secret revolutionary organisation, the Irish Republican Brotherhood, and through her open military organisations, the Irish Volunteers and the Irish Citizen Army, having patiently perfected her discipline, having resolutely waited for the right moment to reveal itself, she now seizes that moment, and, supported by her exiled children in America and by gallant allies in Europe, but relying in the first on her own strength, she

Proclamation of the Irish Republic
Courtesy New York Public Library

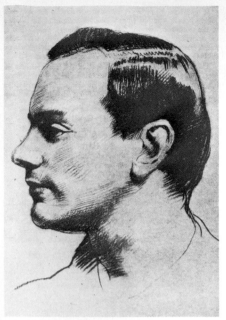

P. H. Pearse

Thomas MacDonagh

Edward Daly

Joseph Mary Plunket

a very devil in jail. Every sort of punishment for his violence had not stopped it. He had smashed furniture, torn off all his clothes and broken handcuffs put on to subdue him. Finally the British gave up trying to break him. They reduced his sentence from five to two years and transferred him to Mountjoy Prison in Dublin. Discipline there was easygoing, and better treatment calmed him. But he was just the sort of man Collins wanted for his plans.

Collins did not take part himself in the jail delivery, but he planned and directed the whole operation. He succeeded in communicating his plan to Fleming. On March 29, 1919, some of his men stood outside Mountjoy Prison. Among them was the Big Fellow's close friend, Joe O'Reilly, with three bicycles.

From inside the jail came a signal. Collins' men threw a rope ladder over the wall. What happened is best told by Joe O'Reilly's report to Collins at a hotel after he had got Fleming safely into hiding.

"Is Fleming out?" Collins demanded.

"The whole jail is out," said O'Reilly.

"What?" cried Collins. "How many?"

"About twenty when I came away."

The Big Fellow burst into uproarious laughter. He went immediately to interview Fleming. All through the evening, Collins kept chuckling as he thought of what the governor of Mountjoy must have thought and said when he found his prison almost empty.

Collins had another daring scheme up his sleeve. He had a good friend, Joe Kavanagh, at Dublin Castle, ready to do him favors, and another, Ned Broy, a young police clerk at detective headquarters. Collins was in touch with both of them. As a result, late one night Broy brought him into headquarters. The two went past the dormitory where the detectives were all soundly sleeping and entered the record room. The Big Fellow spent the rest of the night going over the police files, where his own adventurous activities and those of his friends were written up.

These secret reports showed Collins what the police knew about Irish rebel activities. He discovered that there were British spies even among the secret Irish organizations, and he knew he had to find a way to stop them.

Collins decided to tell the detectives to be careful what they did or take the consequences. The detectives sneered at the warning and decided to get the Big Fellow.

As a result of de Valera's visit to the United States, an organization there called the Friends of Irish Freedom sent three delegates to the Paris Peace Conference. From there they went to Dublin in May, 1919, and were welcomed at a special session of the Dáil Éireann in the Mansion House, the official residence of Dublin's Lord Mayor. Michael Collins attended. After the meeting ended, he and two friends were having lunch when suddenly Joe O'Reilly burst in with word that armed police were advancing on the double to capture the Big Fellow, while the surrounding streets were filled with soldiers.

Collins rushed to the rear entrance and peered out. He saw a detective and a dozen soldiers coming up the lane. O'Reilly found a ladder, and Collins and his friends climbed over a high wall and into an adjoining building.

The Lord Mayor himself opened the front door to let in a host of detectives. O'Reilly, who had not climbed the ladder, was arrested, but then released. When the detectives left, Collins returned in a sorry state, dirty and covered with dust. He sent O'Reilly home for his uniform, since there was to be a public reception that evening in the Mansion House for the American delegates. Collins cleaned himself up and was the only man at the reception in uniform, natty and smart-looking. It made a sensation. That was the way the Big Fellow was. He loved to show off, but after all, he had a right to.

Chapter 10

UNDECLARED WAR and
the BLACK and TANS

IN THE SUMMER of 1919, Britain seemed to have given up trying to subdue Ireland by negotiating a treaty that would enable her to keep a hold on the country even if some sort of independence were granted. Nearly 10,000 armed police of the Royal Irish Constabulary manned barracks in every village and town. Many soldiers equipped with tanks, armored cars, guns and other arms were landed in Dublin in June. It was costing Britain £10,800,000 a year (about $52,000,000 in American money then) to maintain this occupation force.

In spite of this, Ireland continued to consider herself an independent republic. The Dáil Éireann met regularly. It established national arbitration courts, began setting up a consular service to represent it in foreign countries and provided land for farmers who had lost theirs. To help pay the cost of these and other projects, the Dáil asked for a national loan of £250,000 in certificates to be bought by the citizens at five per cent interest.

Ireland was still not completely united. When it was proposed that all Volunteers take an oath not only to the republic but also to the Dáil, Michael Collins and some others objected. They felt that the simple oath all Volunteers took to the republic was enough. As for the secret Irish Republican Brotherhood, which favored continuation of an alliance with Britain by the republic, it remained aloof.

The Volunteers now became the Irish Republican Army (or I.R.A.). Michael Collins held the most important post in it, as director of organization and intelligence. Collins appointed his friend Liam Tobin as his deputy in charge of collecting information about the British government in Ireland and its spies. The Big Fellow's objective was to destroy both.

Tobin, an able intelligence man, set up an office and staff and began to get every scrap of information he could. He also selected a group of daring young men called the Squad. They went about Dublin ready to strike whenever and wherever Collins ordered.

Collins always tried to avoid killing if possible. But Detective-Sergeant Patrick Smith, known as "Dog Smith," was one of the most obnoxious of the police in Dublin. When he ignored several warnings to cease his activities, Collins ordered him shot in July, 1919. Members of the Squad gunned him down outside his house in Drumcondra.

Joe O'Reilly reported the execution to his chief. The Big Fellow, who had been grim and silent for days before he gave the order, strode around the room for ten minutes, swinging his arms and grinding his heels on the floor like a madman. Suddenly he turned on his innocent friend O'Reilly and raged at him.

Arthur Griffith, the moderate, who was Acting President in de Valera's absence, was strongly opposed to such tactics, but he had an unswerving loyalty to the Big Fellow. He did nothing to restrain Collins from continuing such actions.

Britain was still tightening her military grip on Ireland. Before the end of 1919 there were 43,000 British troops in Ireland in addition to the enormous police force. They broke up meetings, raided and searched private houses, disabled printing presses and jailed persons who had Republican literature, often without trial. Among those sentenced to prison were a woman and a priest.

Such actions met with prompt reprisals by Michael Collins and his men. When police and soldiers raided one of his hiding places in September, the Big Fellow barely escaped and the men who were with him were arrested. The next day an especially troublesome detective was shot dead in front of police headquarters.

The house where Collins had set up new headquarters was then raided. He was ready for it, having a light ladder in place through a skylight. As the raiders charged in, he climbed and pulled it up after him and crawled across some roofs to the Standard Hotel. He had already arranged for another ladder to be in place through an open skylight, but to his dismay it was not there. With monkeylike agility he swung himself through the skylight, expecting to drop to a stair landing below. Instead, below him yawned the deep well of the staircase. The Big Fellow had to use all his strength to swing out as far as he could before dropping. He was lucky enough to land on the stairs but was severely bruised as he struck. Nevertheless, he swaggered out of the hotel, called a hackney cab and drove off grinning in spite of his pain.

Next an obscure character named Quinlisk turned up and offered his services. Collins was convinced he could be useful, but the man soon turned against him. Quinlisk insisted that Collins had treated him shamefully, and went to Dublin Castle with an offer to betray the Big Fellow.

A reward of £10,000 had been offered for Collins' capture. Quinlisk set about collecting it. But in trying to locate Collins' whereabouts at the time, he foolishly asked Padraic Fleming. Fleming immediately informed the Big Fellow, who set a trap for Quinlisk.

"Tell Quinlisk I'm staying at my home in Clonakilty," he instructed Fleming. Clonakilty was his native town, southwest of Cork.

Quinlisk went to Clonakilty, but found no trace of Collins. He then went to Cork, where some of the Big Fellow's agents arrested him and sent a message to Collins for permission to kill him. It soon arrived, and they took the traitor to a lonely road outside the city and shot him.

Dublin Castle was still determined to catch Collins. In November, 1919, a short, pudgy, sharp-featured but affable man arrived in Dublin. He said his name was Jameson, though it was not his real one, and he was a smart British secret service agent. Jameson managed to get a letter of introduction to Collins. Joe O'Reilly was immediately suspicious, but the Big Fellow agreed to meet the man. Collins liked Jameson and thought his credentials and offer to aid the Irish cause were genuine.

Save for a foolish mistake, the British might have taken Collins. Jameson arranged a meeting with Collins at Batt O'Connor's house in southeast Dublin. The Big Fellow's faithful aide, Liam Tobin, took the spy there. Meanwhile, a few hundred yards away, the street swarmed with troops and police ready to shoot Collins down.

When the interview was over, Tobin and Jameson left together. Immediately afterward another man came out of the house, got on a bicycle and rode off. Tobin was horrified to see the British and thought it was all up with the Big Fellow. But then it was Jameson's turn to be thrown into consternation. The British made for him and Tobin instead. A detective had reported that it was Collins who had left the house with Jameson. By that time the Big Fellow had safely pedaled away on his bicycle.

Collins chuckled over the mistake that had saved his life, but he planned a reckoning for Mr. Jameson. The spy, not knowing Collins was aware of his treachery, kept in touch with the Big Fellow's men, hoping for another chance to catch him.

At the end of February, 1920, Jameson asked Joe O'Reilly to arrange a meeting with Collins. O'Reilly reported this, and Collins grimly wrote a few lines on a piece of paper and gave it to O'Reilly. It was an order for Jameson's execution.

A meeting place was set. O'Reilly was waiting when Jameson arrived. Then four young men appeared, describing themselves as an escort to take the traitor to Collins. They drove him northward to a remote part of Dublin. There the escort took him into a lane and halted. Jameson then realized he was trapped, but he tried to bluff his way out.

"Oh, you fellows will get hell if anything happens to me," he said. "Collins will deal with you."

"Do you wish to pray?" asked one of the men.

"No."

"We are only doing our duty."

"And I have done mine," replied the traitor. He stood at attention until the escort's guns blazed and he crumpled to the ground.

Early in 1920 a new development that was to result in outright war on the British in Ireland began. Lloyd George had decided that the only way to tame the Irish was to be completely ruthless. In that he made almost as great a mistake as the British government had in allowing General Maxwell to shoot the leaders of the Easter Week uprising. A new force was recruited for Ireland that would become infamous as the Black and Tans, since when they began arriving on March 25, 1920, they wore khaki coats with black trousers and caps.

Winston Churchill, now Secretary of State for War, claimed that they had been carefully selected from a large number of applicants. Churchill is one of England's greatest heroes, but like all men he had his failings. He could be arrogant, disagreeable and unscrupulous. Actually, most of the Black and Tans were unemployable at regular jobs; many were ex-convicts, bullies, the very scum of humanity. They could not be disciplined, and the British command in Ireland made little attempt to do so.

Lumped in with the Black and Tans were a special force of higher caliber known as the Auxiliaries or Cadets. They were supposed to be former officers and were paid double what the ordinary Black and Tans got. The I.R.A. had a certain respect for their fighting abilities, but this did not prevent them from taking revenge on the Auxiliaries for the savagery with which they often treated innocent civilians as well as Irish soldiers.

The task of waging the war on the Black and Tans fell squarely on Michael Collins' shoulders. He accepted it, changing his whole way of life to accomplish the rebels' aim— to make Britain's attempt to subdue Ireland so costly that the

London government would be forced to withdraw completely.

The Big Fellow called on all the powers of his mighty body, will power and keen mind to do this. He gave up smoking and most of his drinking. At his Intelligence Office he spent the mornings clearing up leftover work, going over dispatches, dictating replies to them and reading the Irish and English newspapers. In the afternoon he was out seeing those who were gathering intelligence at various points.

He did relax by going to the racetrack or the theater, yet he managed to keep pace with the endless problems that confronted him.

He had another form of relaxation that was anything but pleasant to his companions. He loved to tease and play practical jokes on them. Often he would start a roughhouse without warning, pushing, wrestling and hurling crockery, furniture or whatever he could grab. He called it "exercise." Once, to escape him, they succeeded in locking him in and piled furniture against the door. When Collins' powerful muscles failed to break down the door, he climbed on a chair and drenched the man nearest the door with the contents of a fire extinguisher through the transom. A close friend and his wife furnished a room for him. Within a week he had wrecked it.

Yet his friends understood that he loved them and that this rough tomfoolery eased the terrible tension he was under. They even forgave his rages, for he did have an ungovernable temper. During these furious outbursts he would taunt his companions cruelly. But suddenly he might embrace them or burst into laughter one moment and tears the next.

The undeclared war was going on. The I.R.A. ambushed

lorries and raided barracks, while the British troops arrested everyone who even looked suspicious.

Cork was a hotbed of rebellion. Tomás MacCurtain had been unanimously elected Lord Mayor of the city. He was also commandant of the Cork brigade of the I.R.A. In the night of March 19, 1920, while police and troops surrounded the area, men with blackened faces burst into MacCurtain's house. They shot him, and he lived only a quarter of an hour. Michael Collins did his best to trace the murderers. He believed he identified several, but he was able to have only one of them killed.

Unafraid, Terence MacSwiney, second in command of the brigade, took over as Lord Mayor. A coroner's jury returned a verdict of "willful murder" against Lloyd George, Lord French and several members of the Royal Irish Constabulary.

MacSwiney was arrested while presiding at a meeting in the Cork City Hall August 12, 1920, and charged with the possession of documents urging the overthrow of the British government. Declaring the British court that tried him illegal, he refused to plead and was imprisoned in Cork.

MacSwiney began a hunger strike. On the third day of it he was put aboard a British warship, taken to England and imprisoned in Brixton Jail. He kept up his fast for seventy-four days. On October 25 he died, his name already famous all over the world.

Seventeen Irishmen were killed in October, 1920, but November was an even blacker month for Ireland. The list of persons, including an eight-year-old child, who were shot or hanged during that time is a long one.

Michael Collins believed that a group of British spies his intelligence men had discovered living as ordinary citizens in Dublin were the most dangerous of all Ireland's enemies.

He ordered them destroyed. On the morning of Sunday, September 21, 1920, some of Collins' men smashed into the houses of fourteen of these secret agents and shot them dead.

British retaliation was almost instantaneous. That afternoon there was a football game in Croke Park, near Drumcondra. A crowd of between six and eight thousand people attended. British troops surrounded the field. The British claimed that they intended to search for arms. But suddenly Black and Tans arrived in lorries and opened fire on the crowd.

They kept firing for ten minutes. There was a wild stampede among the spectators to get away. Twelve men and women were shot dead, and hundreds were wounded, trampled and injured. This Ireland would not forget. They called it Bloody Sunday.

During all this time de Valera was still in the United States. He had planned only a brief stay, but there were complications that kept him there much longer. Arthur Griffith had been Acting President during his absence, but on November 26, 1920, both he and Eóin MacNeill were arrested. For a short time Michael Collins added to his already backbreaking duties those of Acting President of Ireland.

In the United States, de Valera had three chief objectives: to obtain money under what was called the Dáil Éireann External Loan, win recognition of the Irish Republic from the United States government and, if the United States joined the League of Nations, secure American help for that organization's recognition of the new republic.

De Valera secured a commitment for a loan of $100,000 from the Friends of Irish Freedom. This was only about a quarter of the money the organization had collected. One reason for de Valera's prolonged stay in America was that he was drawn into a controversy among the leaders of the Friends. Two of them, John Devoy and Judge Daniel F. Cohalan, wanted the money used for political purposes, especially opposition to the League of Nations. They believed the League would not aid Ireland's cause. Other leaders of the group wanted all the money sent directly to the Dáil Éireann to use as it saw fit. De Valera spent much time trying to gain a compromise between the two factions, but the ill feeling remained.

On October 1, 1919, de Valera set out on a tour that took him throughout the United States. Everywhere he was honored and received with great enthusiasm by immense crowds. Americans liked this American-born Irish President who was doing what great American patriots had done before and during the American Revolution.

It was not until December, 1920, that de Valera sailed for home. Only one of his aims had been fully accomplished. The bond issue for American aid had raised five times as much as the Dáil Éireann had expected. A request for American recognition of free Ireland had been officially presented. Unfortunately, it was not to be granted, but an Irish trade consul had been established in New York. And since the United States did not join the League of Nations, hope for its aid there came to nothing.

In Ireland, meanwhile, Michael Collins' limitless energies had enabled him to handle the £250,000 Republican Bond issue in Ireland magnificently. It was oversubscribed by £40,000. The Irish people had been willing to risk as much as they possibly could so that their cause might succeed.

The undeclared war on Britain was already a bloody one,

but so far it had been confined mostly to bold raids by the I.R.A. on British intelligence agents and some retaliation by the Black and Tans and wholesale arrests of Irish people. The worst was yet to come.

Chapter 11

WAR

BRITAIN'S MAILED FIST began to hammer with all its force early in 1921. Four counties in the far south—Cork, Kerry, Tipperary and Limerick—had already been placed under martial law. Now it was applied to neighboring Wexford, Waterford, Kilkenny and Clare.

In order to execute Irish prisoners legally under the sentence of a court-martial, a state of war had to exist between Britain and Ireland. Mindful that this had not been the case with the leaders of the Easter Week uprising, the government brought the question before the High Court of the King's Bench in London. It ruled that a state of war did exist. Soon afterward five convicted young Irishmen were shot for carrying arms.

Revenge was swift and sure. That very night six British soldiers were shot dead in Cork.

Michael Collins and his men were busy in Dublin. They ambushed more Black and Tans. The British were still hot on the Big Fellow's trail. They often surrounded large areas with troops and scoured the houses for wanted men, hoping the net would catch the biggest and most troublesome fish of all—Michael Collins. He had more narrow escapes, some hairbreadth ones, but always he slipped free.

Black and Tans chased down rebels as a kind of sport, as if they were fox hunting in England. They cruelly humiliated many they caught by forcing them to shout, "God save the King!", spit on pictures of de Valera and drag the tricolor flag of the Irish Republic in the mud.

The highly paid Auxiliaries were the worst. In February, 1921, fifteen I.R.A. men were trapped in a cottage in County Cork. The Irish held their enemies off for two hours by firing through windows until the thatched roof was set afire.

"Surrender!" an Auxiliary officer called out. "You will be properly treated if you do."

The fifteen men came out, unarmed, with their hands up. The "proper" treatment was described later by a survivor, who said the Auxiliaries fell upon them "like wild beasts." Nine were killed, five were wounded and all were looted of everything they had on them.

In County Meath, eleven lorries filled with Auxiliaries came to a liquor shop on March 9.

"We want ammunition," they demanded of the man who was there.

"I have no ammunition," he replied.

With that, they knocked him downstairs, drank some liquor and took all the clothing they could find, soaked it with gasoline in the yard and set it afire. They took liquor whose value was estimated at £100 and ill-treated the man's sister. Two Auxiliaries, at the risk of being killed by their comrades, reported the incident, and several Auxiliaries were suspended.

There were stories of similar brutalities against harmless citizens all over Ireland. In two months, early in 1921, civilians and I.R.A. men killed were estimated at 317, with 285 wounded. The I.R.A. had to be satisfied with killing about 174 and wounding 288.

A man who accepted public office under the Irish government risked his life. In Limerick, during March, the mayor, former mayor and one other public figure were shot on the same night.

Word of these butcheries spread outside Ireland. Even some English newspapers protested it, and Herbert Asquith, the former Prime Minister, and Sir John Simon denounced the British government police in Ireland as murderers.

But the frightfulness went on. Even women were shot or died of wounds caused by the British forces. Meanwhile, Irish relief organizations did a heroic job of feeding and providing shelter for those whose houses had been destroyed. An American organization sent shiploads of food and clothing. The British went as far as they dared in suppressing this aid, but they failed to starve Ireland into submission.

The I.R.A. adopted the best method of fighting the British —guerrilla warfare. They knew the countryside, with its wooded mountains and likely places to set up ambushes and barricades or dig trenches in the roads, while the British did not.

The I.R.A. organized flying columns to conduct swift, daring raids like those of Michael Collins' Squad in Dublin. Soon, in most of western Ireland and its Midlands, the Black and Tans and police were afraid to come out of their barracks except in groups of a hundred or more. The flying columns were forever swooping down on these buildings too, seizing their arms and ammunition. During that spring of 1921, they even captured an enemy airplane and an armored car. And in spite of desperate British efforts to surround the flying columns, the country people were always ready to hide them securely.

In Dublin, Michael Collins was having his troubles, however. For one thing, de Valera was back at the helm. They liked and respected each other and the President considered Collins highly valuable, but his views on defeating Britain did not agree with the Big Fellow's. Soon after his return from America, de Valera, in a statement, reminded the people that the enemy had superior forces and military equipment. He was for a delaying policy, since Ireland could not defeat Britain in an all-out war. If the republic could show endurance and moral resistance, the British would be forced to seek peace sooner or later.

Nevertheless, de Valera understood what Collins had done for Ireland and the strain he had been under. The Big Fellow had much greater difficulties with Cathal Brugha. For one thing, Brugha had been Minister of Defense all along, and had authority over Collins' military actions, of which he did not approve.

The President's cabinet, after his return from America, included Collins as Minister of Finance, Brugha as Minister of Defense and Austin Stack as Minister of Home Affairs. Neither Brugha nor Stack agreed with Collins' methods, and they teamed up against him. Besides, de Valera's statement showed that he wanted more moderation. So for the time being, at least, Collins had less freedom to fight the enemy as he pleased.

De Valera had good reason to feel that his policy was best for Ireland. A new storm of protest against Britain was rising. A number of important British newspapers were exposing what was going on in Ireland. An English nobleman organized the "Peace with Ireland Council." Other titled Englishmen spoke out in Parliament. The Archbishop of Canterbury, head of the Church of England, spoke out strongly. In Scotland and especially in Wales, the people were indignant. And many people abroad contributed money and supplies.

David Lloyd George was an intensely clever, able and sometimes foxy Welshman who became very famous as Prime Minister during and after World War I. But he was a stubborn man, and in spite of all the furor over Britain's treatment of Ireland, he clung obstinately to his plan of subduing the Irish by force.

Other British leaders, however, were working for some sort of solution to the problem. Lloyd George let them go ahead. He was looking for some signs of weakening among the Irish leaders. They were frequently asked to give their opinions on what should be done.

One was Michael Collins. Lloyd George was most anxious to hear the Big Fellow's views, but he stood firm against a personal meeting with a man who ordered policemen shot. Nevertheless, he found out what he wanted to know when Carl Ackerman of the *Philadelphia Public Ledger* interviewed Collins.

Ackerman quoted Collins as follows:

"It is only a question of time until we shall have Ireland cleared of Crown forces."

"What are your terms of settlement?" he was asked.

"Lloyd George has a chance of showing himself to be a great statesman by recognizing the Irish Republic."

"Do you mean a Republic within the British Commonwealth of Nations or outside?"

The Big Fellow did not hesitate an instant: "No, I mean an Irish Republic!"

In discussing the Home Rule Act, which would keep Northern Ireland a part of the British Empire, Collins said, "We do not intend to have Lloyd George put a little red spot on the map of one corner of Ireland and call it part of England, as he does Gibraltar. We want a united Ireland."

De Valera planned to send Collins to America to raise money and obtain arms, organize a boycott of British goods there and perhaps even end the disagreement among the Friends of Irish Freedom. Americans, especially Irish-Americans, had heard of the Big Fellow's fantastic exploits. To see and meet him would be like entertaining a Lancelot in shining armor.

But the plan was dropped when, in April, 1921, an English nobleman came secretly to Ireland under an assumed name to discuss a possible settlement unofficially. He was Lord Derby, a former cabinet member. The President decided that Collins was too valuable a man to be away during Lord Derby's visit.

At the house of one of his friends, de Valera met Lord Derby and they had a long talk. Derby let the President know that Britain might be willing to offer a somewhat better settlement than had previously been proposed. De Valera, for his part, told Lord Derby that no settlement of any kind could be made unless Ireland were given her full freedom.

The Partition Act, passed in 1920 by the British Parliament, but not enforced, was now put into effect. It established a separate government in the six counties of Northern Ireland.

In England, Winston Churchill, now chairman of the Cabinet Committee on Irish Affairs, proposed that 100,000 new special troops be raised and thousands of armored cars equipped. All over southern Ireland areas would be enclosed by barbed wire, and every citizen questioned and every house rummaged for arms and other contraband.

First, however, Churchill was willing to be generous. They

would threaten the action he suggested, but at the same time offer southern Ireland greater self-rule than Home Rule provided. If this were refused, however, Britain should use "the most unlimited exercise of rough-handed force—a tremendous onslaught."

The British cabinet appeared to be ready to go ahead with Churchill's proposals. It was a fearful threat, and at the same time the I.R.A. was having its troubles. In many parts of the country ammunition was running dangerously short. Ireland's climate is normally damp, but 1921 was an unusually dry season. That permitted British armored cars to travel more easily over boggy country roads. The Black and Tans were often able to pursue and surround flying columns.

The British were still hanging and shooting prisoners. It was estimated that between January and June, 1921, the number of captured Republicans killed without trial was 131, while seventeen children, five women and sixteen men were killed by stray bullets.

Nevertheless, in May and June, 1921, the I.R.A. fought on doggedly. In Dublin, Cathal Brugha, with de Valera's reluctant approval, decided to attack Dublin's beautiful Custom House, since the British local government and commissioners' records were stored there; to destroy them would be of great importance.

The attack was made on the afternoon of May 25, 1921, by about 120 members of the Dublin I.R.A. Brigade. They surrounded the building and forced the staff to leave. The building, restored today, was then set afire. It burned all night, and its huge copper dome collapsed. Some of the raiders were accidentally trapped in the fire and died, and about seventy of them were arrested.

Because of the ammunition shortage, burning and destruction were being used more and more by the I.R.A. When the Black and Tans retaliated on the property of Republicans, the I.R.A. counterattacked and destroyed houses of persons known to be aiding the British. And although the Irish people were living under great strain and privation and, because of the lack of funds, could not always obtain relief, they were still determined to keep their free republic.

Then, without warning, there came a sudden change in London. There had been no indication of an alteration in British policy; at a cabinet meeting on May 12, 1921, nine ministers, including Lloyd George, opposed seeking a truce with Ireland against five in favor of it. But less than a month later something happened to alter that decision.

Good King George V, beloved by the English people, came to Northern Ireland to open its Parliament. In his speech he said:

I speak from a full heart when I pray that my coming to Ireland today may prove to be the first step towards the end of strife among her people, whatever the race or creed.

In that hope I appeal to all Irishmen to pause, to stretch out the hand of forbearance and conciliation, to forgive and forget and to join in making for the land they love a new era of peace, contentment and good will.

It is my earnest desire that in Southern Ireland too, there may, ere long, take place a parallel to what is now passing in this hall; that there a similar occasion may present itself, and a similar ceremony be performed. . . .

The future lies in the hands of my Irish people themselves. May this historic gathering be the prelude of the day in which the Irish people, North and South, under one Parliament or two, as those Parliaments may themselves decide, shall work together in common love for Ireland and upon the sure foundation of mutual justice and respect.

When the King returned to London, he was met by the Prime Minister and received a tremendous ovation from thousands along his route to Buckingham Palace. It was plain that the people approved of his appeal for peace.

On the very afternoon of the day the King spoke in Belfast, President de Valera was in the grounds of a house into which he had moved, since he was still keeping out of sight of the British. An open lorry carrying a special squad of soldiers drew up at the gate. De Valera saw them and tried to escape through a rear gate, but it was locked. They arrested him at gunpoint. But the next morning he was released without explanation after spending the night in a room at Portobello Barracks.

For three days he had no clue as to what had happened. Then he received a letter from Prime Minister Lloyd George. It proposed that they meet to discuss peace.

Chapter 12

THE TREATY

EAMON DE VALERA was doubtful of Lloyd George's letter. He knew the little Welshman could be wily, and he suspected a plan to secure Partition, separating Northern Ireland from the southern part.

Nevertheless, as Lloyd George had suggested, he invited representatives to meet with him at the Dublin Mansion House, including five Unionists, who favored keeping Ireland as part of the British Empire. Among these was Sir James Craig, Prime Minister of Northern Ireland, the only one who refused to attend.

The Republican leaders included Arthur Griffith, Robert Barton, Eóin MacNeill, Eamonn Duggan and Michael Staines. All had been released from prison by the British, although thirty-four members of the Dáil Éireann were still in jail.

As a result of the meeting, de Valera telegraphed Lloyd George that he was ready to meet him for discussions. The Prime Minister replied that he would be happy to see him, with any of his leaders he would like to bring with him.

Before the delegation left, a truce was arranged in a con-

ference with officers of the British army in Ireland. Both
sides agreed to stop all military activity, and the truce became effective on July 11, 1921.

To most of the Irish population the truce meant that peace
had come. They celebrated so joyously and wildly, lighting
bonfires and demanding release of the Irish prisoners still
held, that the I.R.A. had to be stern in cooling off the excited
people lest the truce be violated.

In Northern Ireland there was no rejoicing. The strong
Protestant majority there wanted no separation from Britain,
and they vented their displeasure on the Catholics there.
Belfast, like Dublin, had its Bloody Sunday on July 10, 1921,
when Protestant mobs burned 161 Catholic houses, killed 15
persons and injured 68.

President de Valera's party, which included Arthur Griffith, Austin Stack, Robert Barton, Count Plunkett and Erskine Childers, left Ireland on July 12. Lloyd George received
them with great courtesy and amiability in his official residence at 10 Downing Street in London on July 14.

They talked for three hours. After a second meeting, Lloyd
George's proposal for a treaty was given to de Valera.

It was a great disappointment. Britain offered Ireland an
opportunity to "take her place in the great association of free
nations over which His Majesty reigns." This was no offer of
a free Irish Republic, but one of becoming a British Dominion, and while Ireland was to have a free hand in taxation
and finance, there was paragraph after paragraph of restric-
tions. Britain wanted naval bases in Ireland, rights to recruit
soldiers, a limit on the Irish armed forces, free trade between
Britain and Ireland, financial help from Ireland in paying
Britain's enormous war debt and other demands. Also, Northern Ireland was to have its own government.

De Valera, after discussions with his party, saw Lloyd George and rejected the proposal in no uncertain terms.

The Prime Minister was ready with his answer, a menacing threat: "Do you realize that this means war? Do you realize that the responsibility for it will rest on your shoulders alone?"

"No, Mr. Lloyd George," returned de Valera stoutly, "if you insist on attacking us, it is you, not I, who will be responsible, because you will be the aggressor."

"I could put a soldier in Ireland for every man, woman and child in it," retorted Lloyd George.

"Very well. But you would have to keep them there."

The Prime Minister made another threat he hoped would be effective: "I will publish these terms immediately for the Irish people to see. I will leave the Irish people the chance of knowing what is being offered them."

"Go ahead, but I thought that nothing would be published unless we both agreed."

Lloyd George brushed this aside as a trivial matter.

"So I must assume that is how you keep your promises," de Valera reproached him. "But have your way. You publish your terms, and I will publish my refusal of them."

Both angry men had risen from the table. De Valera left the British proposal lying there. Before he left, the two did agree that the truce should be extended. And that evening the Irish President sent back a messenger for the proposed treaty so he could study it before making a final reply.

De Valera and his party then returned to Ireland. On August 10 the President sent Lloyd George his cabinet's rejection of the terms. He also outlined what sort of settlement they would be willing to recommend to the Dáil. He spoke of the "claim advanced by your government to an interference with our affairs, and to a control which we cannot admit."

Lloyd George replied in a long letter which included these words: ". . . We must direct your attention to one point upon which you lay some emphasis and upon which no British government can compromise—namely, the claim that we should acknowledge the right of Ireland to secede from her allegiance to the King. No such right can ever be acknowledged by us."

The fate of Ireland was going to rest on a solution of that very point.

The final acceptance or rejection of the British terms was to be determined by a vote of the Dáil Éireann when it met on August 16. Meanwhile, all the members of the Dáil still imprisoned were released except one, Séan MacEóin, who had been convicted of murder.

De Valera then issued a public statement in which he said that if MacEóin remained in prison, all negotiations would be broken off. They let MacEóin go at once.

The Dáil consisted of 130 Republican members, 6 Nationalists and 44 Unionist representatives from Northern Ireland, who as usual refused to attend. A great crowd assembled outside the Mansion House when the Dáil met there.

President de Valera addressed the members and explained what they were called upon to decide. There was much discussion, and it was a week before the British proposal came up for a vote. It was rejected with only one member voting for it.

There followed a long correspondence between de Valera and Lloyd George in which the Prime Minister used all his eloquence and persuasiveness to get an acceptance. Meanwhile, in England, new threats of reopening the war were being made. But in October, 1921, Lloyd George sent a new invitation to a conference in London. De Valera had won a point.

It was somewhat of a shock to his cabinet when the President told the members he did not wish to be one of the negotiators in London. Several felt strongly that he should go. De Valera did not fully explain his reasons at that time, but several months later he gave them in a letter to one of his principal American supporters. The main reason was that he knew that the delegates, in dealing with Lloyd George, might have to make some concessions. It would never do for the people to have any suspicions that the President was letting them down.

In case "external association" had to be yielded to the British, it would be important for de Valera to be at home, where he could use his powerful influence to gain acceptance of it. "External association" meant that Ireland would be ready to become an external associate of the British Commonwealth of Nations. Under it, Ireland's independence would not be endangered, nor would she be requested to take part in any British action against other nations. But even this concession was not going to be easy for some of the Irish leaders, who wanted absolute freedom, to swallow.

The next task was to select the delegates to this crucial conference. De Valera proposed Arthur Griffith and, to balance his moderate position, Michael Collins. Both agreed to go. Cathal Brugha and Austin Stack, however, refused. Robert Barton agreed to go. All these were cabinet ministers. As legal advisers, two lawyers who were members of the Dáil were selected. Four high-ranking leaders were chosen as secretaries. The Dáil approved all the appointments.

In view of what had happened in London, one article in the instructions given the Envoys Plenipotentiary, as they were officially called, was of the greatest importance. It said that the complete text of a draft treaty which would then be placed before the Dáil for approval must be submitted by the delegates to Dublin before they signed it, to obtain the cabinet's approval.

The Irish leaders had already drawn up a draft treaty which was acceptable to them as the basis for a settlement with Britain. It provided that the British Commonwealth should recognize Ireland as a sovereign and independent state and give up all claim to interference with Irish affairs, but that Ireland would agree to become an external associate of the British Commonwealth.

The envoys arrived in London on October 9 to be welcomed at the railway station by a vast, cheering crowd which appeared to include most of the Irish residents of England who lived anywhere near the capital. The peace conference began at 10 Downing Street on the morning of October 11.

There were many problems to be discussed and settled. While the Irish envoys had to remember that what they had agreed to was to be approved in Dublin beforehand, Lloyd George had to keep in mind the political opposition he would face when a treaty came before the House of Commons for approval.

The two toughest questions concerned the form of Irish allegiance to the Crown and the problem of Northern Ireland. Regarding the first, Arthur Griffith, in a report to de Valera October 24, said that both Lloyd George and Churchill were insistent on Irish allegiance to the British Crown. "If we come to agreement on all other points," he wrote, "I would recommend some form of association with the Crown."

De Valera's reply was firm: ". . . There can be no question of our asking the Irish people to enter an arrangement which would make them subject to the Crown, or demand for their allegiance to the British King. If war is the only alternative, we can only face it. . . ."

Griffith, Collins and another envoy, Eamonn Duggan, were irate. They felt that the President was interfering with their freedom of action. Griffith wrote an indignant letter to de Valera which the others signed.

De Valera's reply was conciliatory, saying he had no intention of interfering beyond the terms of the envoys' instructions, and after that he toned down his suggestions and advice. This may have had an effect on the delegates that was to cause trouble later. Yet in Dublin the cabinet members discussed the question of allegiance and agreed that it could not be yielded, even if it came to all-out war.

The Northern Ireland question seemed equally insurmountable. Sir James Craig stood like a rock in his insistence that the six northeast counties must remain with the British Empire. It began to look as if the peace conference had reached a deadlock and would fail. The only thing left for Britain would then be to make intensive war on Ireland. In Ireland, de Valera began a tour of inspection with Cathal Brugha and General Richard Mulcahy, chief of staff, to counties Limerick, Clare and Galway to see that military installations there were in readiness, but he had to cut the trip short. He received word that the envoys were bringing the final British offers.

De Valera could not see how they could possibly be accepted. As he wrote later to his American friend, Joe McGarrity, they amounted to Ireland's becoming a British Dominion with an oath of allegiance to the King put into the Irish Constitution, and recognition of the King as chief executive of Ireland.

De Valera also wrote that Griffith gave *"an express under-*

standing that he would not sign a document accepting allegiance but would bring it back and refer the matter to Dáil Éireann. This made us all satisfied; we were certain for our part that Dáil Éireann would reject it."

What de Valera did not know was that in private talks with Lloyd George, Arthur Griffith had been giving the Prime Minister assurances that he could not possibly keep under the instructions to the envoys. Michael Collins agreed with Griffith's idea of yielding to Britain on becoming a Dominion, but in Collins' case he seems to have had the idea that the settlement would be a temporary one. He knew that if the peace conference failed, British might would overwhelm Ireland. He respected that might. Why not make the best settlement possible and then work to find a way to gain full independence?

Ireland's immediate future was decided on December 6, 1921. Lloyd George had Arthur Griffith where he wanted him. The other delegates did not know that Griffith had promised the Prime Minister he would sign the draft of the treaty which was presented to the Irish envoys at a meeting that day.

Lloyd George had a paper Griffith had given him on November 13, agreeing to sign. At the meeting he charged Griffith with intending to break his promise.

"I have never let a man down in my whole life, and I never will," Griffith replied.

"Do I understand, Mr. Griffith, that though everyone else refuses, you will nevertheless agree to sign?"

"Yes, that is so, Mr. Prime Minister."

The other delegates were staggered. Under the proposed treaty, Northern Ireland would continue to be a part of Britain, and members of the Dáil Éireann would take an oath of allegiance to the King. Why had Griffith, a coleader of the envoys, disregarded the instructions they had been given in Dublin?

That evening the envoys met to make their decision. Three, including Michael Collins, agreed to sign. Barton at first refused until it was pointed out to him that he would bring war upon the Irish people. And so it was done—and Lloyd George had won what he had set out to gain.

Why did Arthur Griffith make the secret promise? The best explanation seems to be that he felt sure that the Dáil Éireann would never ratify the treaty and that this would delay war and perhaps gain a better settlement.

The first word that de Valera received came when he met Cathal Brugha and Austin Stack before a ceremony over which he was to preside at the Mansion House the evening of December 7.

"Any news?" the President asked the two cabinet ministers.

"Yes," said Stack.

"Good or bad?"

"Bad."

Then Stack handed de Valera a copy of an evening newspaper containing the story and the provisions of the treaty. Stack wrote later that, as the President read it, "at that moment he appeared to me to be an almost broken man."

The next morning the cabinet members who had remained in Ireland met with de Valera, who announced he would demand the resignations of the three cabinet members in the delegation—Griffith, Collins and Barton. But he was persuaded to wait until the three had a chance to tell their side of the story. De Valera did issue a proclamation, however, saying that he could not recommend acceptance of the treaty either to the Dáil Éireann or the people of the country.

The next day Arthur Griffith also issued a statement. In it

he said, "I believe the treaty will lay the foundation of peace and friendship between the two nations. What I have signed I will stand by, in the belief that the end of the conflict of centuries is at hand."

All members of the Dáil Éireann who had taken the Republican oath were called to meet on December 14. But some of the leaders of the Irish Republican Brotherhood, who had taken the oath, met before that date and decided to throw their strong influence in favor of the treaty's acceptance by the Dáil. They were at least partly swayed by Michael Collins' signing of the treaty, since he had always been active in the Brotherhood.

The British Parliament was the first to ratify the treaty. It passed the House of Commons by a majority of 343 and the House of Lords by 119 votes.

There was long debate when the Dáil Éireann assembled. The first sessions were private; then, on December 19, they were opened to the public. The President had already opposed the treaty and suggested that a revised one be drafted and submitted to the British.

Then Arthur Griffith proposed a resolution to be voted on, approving the treaty. Séan MacEóin seconded him.

Michael Collins spoke for the treaty. His feelings were bitter because someone had called him a traitor. His speech showed that he deeply resented the blame that had been put on the envoys to the peace conference. "I signed it because I would not be one of those to commit the people to war without the Irish people committing themselves to war," he said.

Austin Stack supported de Valera in opposing the treaty. Robert Barton spoke, but he did not commit himself one way or the other. Countess Markievicz bitterly opposed the treaty. She jabbed sharply at Michael Collins, infuriating him by suggesting that perhaps he wanted to marry Princess Mary of England.

The debate went on and on. The President's cabinet was badly split on the question, and de Valera felt that this made it impossible for him to carry out his duties as chief executive to preserve the Irish Republic. On January 6, 1922, he resigned, but was persuaded to withdraw his resignation on condition that a motion to approve the treaty should be voted upon within twenty-four hours.

Before the vote was taken, Cathal Brugha made a strong speech against the treaty. Griffith replied with a denunciation of all those who opposed it.

Then came the vote. Sixty-four voted for approval of the treaty and fifty-seven against it. Thus it was adopted by a majority of only seven. President de Valera again submitted his resignation, which was accepted by the Dáil Éireann by a majority of just two votes. Arthur Griffith was then elected President of the Irish Republic.

The stage was now set for a bloody and disgraceful struggle in Ireland—civil war.

Chapter 13

CIVIL WAR

UNDER THE TREATY, Ireland was to be ruled by a Provisional Government until an election could be held and a permanent government installed. At the same time, the people would indicate by their votes whether they approved the treaty and a new constitution.

Although Arthur Griffith, as President, was the head of Dáil Éireann, Michael Collins was chosen chairman of the Provisional Government. On January 16, 1922, Dublin Castle was turned over to him by the British Lord Lieutenant of Ireland. With that, the British began pulling their troops out of the twenty-six counties of southern Ireland.

The regiments made a brave show of their departure, some for still-British Northern Ireland, the rest for England. They marched out with flags flying and their bands playing. But the show the Irish people enjoyed the most was the departure of the Black and Tans and Auxiliaries and the disbanding of the Royal Irish Constabulary.

The first indication of serious dissension in the new Irish regime began within the Irish Republican Army. Its predecessor, the Volunteers, had been independent, electing its

147

own executive as its head. With the change of name, however, it had been controlled by the Dáil. Now some of its leaders wanted to change it back to the old system, no longer responsible to the Dáil.

These anti-treaty men asked that a convention be held to settle the question. But General Mulcahy, as chief of staff, demanded that the I.R.A. continue to obey the Dáil. However, it was agreed that an Army Convention should be held within two weeks.

Before it could take place, the Second Division of the I.R.A.—located in the province of Munster, which takes in Counties Cork, Kerry, Limerick and Clare in southwestern Ireland—took things into its own hands. This division decided to become independent. It was the beginning of a serious rift that would soon shake all of southern Ireland.

The split continued to widen. The most influential officers of the I.R.A. command were largely supporters of the treaty and were able to lay the foundations of the Irish army it provided for. Officers at I.R.A. headquarters who opposed the treaty found themselves replaced by pro-treaty men.

For a time, on the surface, little seemed changed. The men of the pro-treaty army wore the same green uniforms and badge they had had in 1916, were called Volunteers even though they were paid and flew the tricolor flag. When a detachment of this army marched past the City Hall on the way to occupy Beggars Bush Barracks, Michael Collins stood on the steps to receive their salute, even though this was the Dáil's, not the Provisional Government's army.

But soon men began to resign from the pro-treaty army. Even more deserted, taking their guns with them and joining units of an anti-treaty army which was the beginning of a new I.R.A.

Meanwhile, for weeks on end, Eamon de Valera was touring all Ireland to speak against the treaty. Pro-treaty speakers who claimed that the treaty gave the Irish the opportunity to achieve freedom later on got an answer. De Valera warned his hearers that if they accepted the treaty and later tried to achieve full freedom, they would do so over the dead bodies of their own countrymen, the soldiers of the Irish government the treaty provided for establishing. De Valera also formed an opposition group, the League of the Republic, of which he was president.

While the British troops were still being evacuated from Ireland, violence erupted in Northern Ireland. The root of the trouble was just what was to cause bitterness for many years afterward—persecution of and discrimination against Catholics by many of the much greater population of Protestants there.

On the border—not yet definitely established—between the separated counties there were raids and skirmishes between Ulster troops supported by British units and the I.R.A. in February, 1922. Later there was violence in Belfast in which there were 138 casualties, including the deaths of several Catholic children by a bomb thrown among them. With that, Britain suspended the evacuation of troops from southern Ireland. The treaty was in serious danger.

Nevertheless, the British went ahead with a bill to establish a permanent Irish government. Griffith sent Michael Collins to London, where the Big Fellow spent much time with Winston Churchill ironing out details. As soon as Parliament had passed the bill, the elections could be held in Ireland.

By this time the I.R.A. was really two armies, with entire brigades and divisions definitely either pro-treaty or anti-treaty, each occupying barracks evacuated by the British. Small skirmishes took place between them in which arms, ammunition and lorries were captured by one side or the other. On March 2 the Republican, or anti-treaty, I.R.A. in Dublin was supplied with a large cargo of arms bought in Germany.

The I.R.A. held its convention on March 26. It passed a resolution reaffirming its allegiance to the Irish Republic and placing itself under the temporary control of sixteen representatives called the Executive. Two days later the Executive announced that the authority of the Provisional Government's Minister of Defense and its chief of staff would no longer be obeyed. The I.R.A. was now definitely an anti-treaty army.

The Provisional Government retaliated by giving an account of the convention's action and the names of the sixteen members of the Executive to the newspapers. Only one, the *Freeman's Journal,* printed it. On the night of March 30, I.R.A. raiders wrecked the paper's office.

That same day, members of the I.R.A.'s First Division staged a daring sea hijacking at Cobh. The small freighter *Upnor* was to sail for England with a cargo of small arms and ammunition from an evacuated British barracks. The I.R.A. men planned to intercept the vessel at sea in a launch, but to their chagrin the small boat was not there. So they seized a tug, hauled her skipper out of a pub and forced him to take them out.

The *Upnor* had two escorts, but the I.R.A. hoisted British colors as they came alongside the freighter and the other two ships sailed on unsuspectingly. The raiders boarded the freighter and ran her into a bay a little east of Cobh. There eighty lorries they had commandeered were waiting. Loaded with the loot, the trucks chugged off just as a British destroyer nosed in to see what was going on. The I.R.A. got a large stock of rifles, revolvers, machine guns, hand grenades and ammunition.

Open civil war came nearer. The Republican forces lacked money, which was seized in raids on post offices all over Ireland. Then, on May 1, 1922, with the approval of the Executive, organized raids were carried out on branches of the Provisional Government's Bank of Ireland in which nearly £50,000 was taken. The raiders politely left receipts for the money to show that the I.R.A. intended to pay it back. And Republican army posts were provisioned with seized stores of food.

There was still no bitterness. When Republican troops seized a number of buildings in Kilkenny, they were driven out by two hundred Provisional Government troops from Dublin, but then were allowed to occupy certain posts there. In Dublin the I.R.A. succeeded in seizing several strategic buildings, but there was no fighting.

The British had been supplying the Provisional Government with arms. When the act known as the Irish Free State (Agreement) Bill was passed, the London government considered that this was now legal and on April 12 Churchill announced that 4,000 rifles, 2,200 revolvers and six machine guns, with the necessary ammunition, had been furnished to the Provisional Government.

On both sides efforts were being made for peace, though nothing came of them for a time. The leaders felt that if an agreement between de Valera and Collins could be reached, civil war could be avoided. The two finally got together for conferences and at last they signed a pact stating that the coming elections should not be considered as deciding the question of the treaty, but they agreed to set up a coalition government in the Dáil Éireann with both Republicans and the Treaty Party represented. This coalition would then seek to create peace.

It might have worked save that the pact between the two was as brittle as paper-thin glass. Before the election Collins made a speech in Cork in which he said, "You understand fully what you have to do, and I depend upon you to do it." It was a direct appeal to elect government supporters to the Dáil, and it shattered the pact with de Valera.

As the elections in Ireland approached, the new constitution was not ready so that the people could read it well beforehand and decide whether to vote for candidates for the Dáil who would accept it. The Irish committee preparing it finally made three drafts, all of which they felt would be acceptable, and sent them to England.

Since all the drafts practically ignored the King, the British cabinet members were indignant. Lloyd George went to work on a revision which contained an oath of allegiance to the King that Dáil Éireann members must take, and gave the King power to veto any law passed by the Dáil.

It was the morning of election day before the new constitution was published in the Dublin newspapers. People who lived at any great distance from the city did not see it before voting. Most voted for pro-treaty candidates, believing that the new constitution would establish a real republic.

In the election, 58 pro-treaty and 35 anti-treaty deputies were elected to the Dáil, along with 35 men of other parties, all more or less favorable to the treaty. It seemed inevitable for Ireland to accept the constitution that would keep her still firmly under Britain's thumb.

Then something happened that brought the dissension between the pro-treaty and anti-treaty forces to a crisis. In London, Sir Henry Wilson, a powerful representative of the Northern Ireland government and its military adviser, was shot dead on June 22 on the doorstep of his home by two young Irishmen. They were captured, tried, convicted and executed, but neither said a word to implicate any Irish organization.

Nevertheless, the British took prompt and stern action. Among the places in Dublin occupied by I.R.A. troops was the Four Courts, under Rory O'Connor, the Executive's director of engineering. It was well known that these troops had discussed an attack on the British soldiers still in Dublin. Lloyd George wrote Michael Collins a strong letter telling him he must have the Four Courts evacuated at once or the treaty would be presumed to have been violated and there would be serious consequences.

The Provisional Government tried to delay attacking the Four Courts until the new Dáil Éireann met on June 30 to authorize it. But orders were meanwhile issued in London for the British troops still in the Dublin area to attack the Four Courts themselves. So the Irish cabinet decided it would wait no longer.

At 3:40 A.M. on June 28, 1922, the Provisional Government sent an ultimatum to Rory O'Connor. The Four Courts must be evacuated in twenty minutes. When nothing happened by 4 A.M., Provisional Government troops opened fire on the Four Courts with artillery borrowed from the British.

That morning the people of Dublin awoke to the roar of cannon and the chatter of machine guns. Ireland's terrible Civil War had begun.

Chapter 14

BROTHER AGAINST BROTHER

THE PHRASE "brother against brother" has often been used to describe the Irish Civil War, and in a sense it was true. All Ireland was divided, and good and old friends, if not brothers, fought each other.

Liam Lynch, who had been a commandant in the I.R.A., was chosen that morning of June 28, 1922 as its chief of staff. He sent the men in the Four Courts a message that he was going to rouse the country in behalf of the Republic, and then issued a proclamation to the citizens. He urged them all to rally to the support of the Republic.

De Valera also issued a statement blaming the English for the trouble. In it he said:

"The men who are now being attacked by the forces of the Provisional Government are those who refuse to obey the order to yield—preferring to die. They are the best and bravest of our nation and would most loyally have obeyed the will of the Irish people freely expressed, but are not willing that Ireland's independence should be abandoned under the lash of an alien government."

Commandant Oscar Traynor, of the I.R.A.'s Dublin Brigade, had mobilized his unit and seized several buildings around the Four Courts and in other parts of the city. However, the posts occupied just across the river to the south were taken by the Provisional Government's army, and its artillery was pounding the Four Courts walls. Traynor hoped to get 10,000 men from the countryside who would be able to seize Dublin and maintain peace there, but these men were mobilizing for action in their own districts.

Committees of citizens strove in vain to settle the trouble. Traynor was willing to withdraw if his men were allowed to keep their arms; the Provisional Government, Arthur Griffith and Michael Collins insisted that the arms be surrendered.

On the following day, June 29, the Government troops assaulted the Four Courts and managed to enter part of the building. The Republicans were in trouble and that night attempted to fight their way out, but they gave up when their one machine gun failed. The next morning the building caught fire and, while the men in it were trying to move their store of explosives to a safer area, blew up.

By afternoon, after more explosions, the Four Courts was an inferno, and the men in it were forced to yield to the Provisional Government's terms—unconditional surrender. The I.R.A. men, over a hundred of them, were imprisoned in Mountjoy except for six who escaped on the way there. One was Ernest O'Malley, a member of the Executive, who would be heard from later on.

Next the Government troops closed in on the headquarters of the Dublin Brigade in several hotels in Sackville Street. Their guns pulverized one after another of these buildings until the I.R.A. leaders and the garrison were holed up in one that was left. A plan was then made to save the leaders so they could go around the country to organize resistance in the form of guerrilla warfare.

On Sunday, July 2, part of the headquarters garrison went out under a flag of truce and surrendered. De Valera, Traynor, Austin Stack and several other Republican leaders remained. The next day they crept out, afraid that at any moment the enemy would pounce on them, but to their astonishment no Government troops appeared. They went to concealment in a house where they were expected.

Tough little Cathal Brugha, who had fought like a wildcat in 1916 and survived fourteen bullet wounds, remained in the hotel with seventeen men and three women to care for the wounded. Their orders were to fight until they could no longer stay in the building and then surrender. Twice on Tuesday, July 4, Traynor sent Brugha an order to surrender, but the door was locked against his messenger. By evening, however, the hotel was ablaze and the walls were about to collapse. At Brugha's order those who had stayed went out and surrendered. Suddenly they discovered their leader had not come with them. Then they saw his slight, wiry figure in the doorway, firing at the Government troops with a revolver in each hand. Both his own men and the enemy shouted, "Surrender!"

"No!" Brugha cried. He lunged forward, still firing, and fell dead under a volley of bullets.

That was the end of the fighting in Dublin. Sixty men on both sides had been killed and about three hundred wounded. This time, unlike the situation in 1916, it was the west side of Sackville Street that was in ruins.

From then on the I.R.A. chose the wisest course in fighting the Civil War—largely guerrilla warfare, which would have a better chance for success than the fighting in 1916. Each section of the Republican army was to operate in its own area. Most of the fighting took place in southwestern and western Ireland, the wilder and more mountainous parts of the country, where the Republicans were strongest.

Ernest O'Malley, one of the six who had escaped after the Four Courts surrender, went south and formed the Southeastern Command of the I.R.A. He captured Enniscorthy in County Wexford and garrisoned barracks in neighboring towns. Presently he was appointed assistant chief of staff of the I.R.A.

Liam Lynch took a force from County Cork and went to Limerick, where he occupied part of the city, but after fighting Government forces for about a week he was forced to withdraw. The fighting went on in County Limerick, however, and the I.R.A. seized arms from many prisoners they captured and then released.

Lynch moved to the southeast with some of his staff to Clonmel in Tipperary. De Valera, a fighting man again, joined him there. But when Lynch attempted to occupy the town of Thurles, his men were driven off and many captured. Lynch then established headquarters at Fermoy in County Cork.

The I.R.A. was in almost complete control of the far south of Ireland, below a line extending from Waterford in the southeast to Limerick at the mouth of the River Shannon, well up the southwest coast.

In western Ireland the I.R.A. had occupied Ennis in County Clare. With small armed columns they captured Provisional Government posts and patrols and thus increased their stock of arms and ammunition. They also captured an armored car named the *Ballinalee,* which became famous.

The *Ballinalee*'s activities were in County Sligo. As was

the case in many places in Ireland, the town of Sligo was occupied by both I.R.A. and Government forces. By June 30 it became evident that a battle between them was shaping up.

General Séan McEóin, of the Provisional Government army, arrived in Sligo. The I.R.A. had been superior in numbers there, but his coming seems to have convinced them that he had large Government reinforcements with him. That night of June 30, the I.R.A. men burned their barracks and got out.

Actually, McEóin was on his way to his command headquarters at Athlone, some distance to the south. He had not known of the Civil War, but reports reaching him showed that it had begun all over the country. He returned to Athlone, but so much trouble developed in and around Sligo that he decided a very strong Republican stronghold in the barracks at Boyle must be taken. Government troops had already occupied the workhouse there, but the I.R.A. placed men in houses commanding it, put telephone and telegraph communications out of order and blocked the roads for miles around with felled trees.

Early on July 2 they attacked the workhouse, but were driven back. There was savage hand-to-hand fighting in the streets. Then rifles and machine guns opened up. The battle went on all day until, at about seven o'clock, Provisional Government reinforcements sent by McEóin arrived, along with the *Ballinalee.*

The armored car was a terror to the Republicans. It cruised about routing them from one post after another. The I.R.A. was forced to abandon the barracks, which were in flames. This sort of thing went on for two days, but by July 5 the Provisional Government forces were in full control of the Boyle area.

Next the *Ballinalee* went to Sligo and patrolled the streets for several days. On July 6 it took part in an attack on barracks occupied by a police force the I.R.A. had organized. These police were soon driven out, but two civilians were accidentally killed in the action.

The Republicans were itching to capture the *Ballinalee* somehow. They tried it on July 10, but were beaten off. Then, two days later, they laid a well-planned ambush for the monster.

It was set up in the greatest secrecy near Collooney, a few miles south of Sligo, on the road to Sligo from a Provisional Government post where the *Ballinalee* was kept.

Early on the morning of July 12, a force of Government troops left there in a lorry, escorted by the armored car and bound for Sligo. As they approached the place of ambush at a place called Dooney Rock, they were halted by a road block. The I.R.A. men then opened fire, killing the commanding officer of the force, who was in the lorry.

Foolishly, for some reason, the captain of the *Ballinalee* got out. The ambushers swarmed in on the car and captured it, though not without a hard fight.

To the Republicans the *Ballinalee* was like a new toy, and they not only used it to advantage but had great fun with it. On July 16 it rampaged into Sligo, escorting a force on foot. The streets were crowded with people, and there was a stampede for safety. Provisional Government soldiers who were raiding houses were seized in the streets, and a lorry loaded with their supplies was captured. With the town under full Republican control, the *Ballinalee* remained overnight and then vanished. But McEóin threw reinforcements into the town and regained control.

The *Ballinalee* continued its devastating ramblings all

over the area. Early on August 4 it roared back into Sligo and raked the streets with fire for an hour and a half until the Provisional Government garrison surrendered.

Much more action lay ahead of the *Ballinalee*. Meanwhile, the Republican forces were keeping a tight hold on most of the far south. They guarded approach routes by destroying bridges, digging trenches in roads and setting up ambushes along the steep, narrow passes in that mountain country. But disaster lay ahead.

In August, Provisional Government forces superior in numbers and arms moved in on the southern Republican strongholds. Towns began to fall to the invaders—Waterford, Carrick-on-Suir, Tipperary and Cahir. In other places the I.R.A. held on, but the Provisional Government began sending in troops by sea to attack from the south. Tralee, on the coast in County Kerry, fell. On August 10 the invaders entered Cork City; on the same day, Fermoy, I.R.A. headquarters where de Valera was then, was taken, and the Republican forces fled to the hills after burning their barracks. The Provisional Government was now in full military control of Ireland.

Yet the fighting went on as bitterly as ever. August, 1922, was a black month for both the Republicans and the Provisional Government.

Harry Boland, though a Republican a good and long-time friend of both de Valera and Michael Collins, was sleeping in a hotel at Skerries, on the coast a little north of Dublin. At about two in the morning a large group of Government soldiers with an armored car surrounded the hotel. Six of them entered Boland's room. He woke in time to dash for freedom, but was shot down. On August 2 he died in a hospital. When Michael Collins heard of it he wept bitterly, as he had when he was told of Cathal Brugha's death.

Collins wept too when his associate through the years, Arthur Griffith, died suddenly. Griffith had been ill, suffering from overwork, but seemed to have recovered. As he was leaving his office on August 12, he collapsed. A blood vessel in his brain had broken, and he died in a few hours.

With Harry Boland's death during that ominous month of August, Michael Collins became commander in chief of the Provisional Government army. Once Cork City was taken and the Government position in the south was secure, Collins set out to inspect the posts taken from the I.R.A.

While Collins was marching in Arthur Griffith's funeral procession, before leaving Dublin, two more of his friends— Reginald Dunne and Joseph O'Sullivan—had only hours to live. In Wandworth Jail in England these two men were awaiting execution by hanging for the shooting of Sir Henry Wilson. It has been charged, though never proved, that the Big Fellow ordered the killing. But if he did, Dunne and O'Sullivan never betrayed him, and in any event Collins was heavy-hearted over their coming deaths.

Collins was at the lowest ebb of his life. He stopped at Clonmel on his way to Cork. That night he had a bad chill and still felt very sick in the morning, but he was determined to go on to Cork.

"You're a fool to go," said one of his friends.

"Ah, whatever happens to me, my own fellow countrymen won't kill me," Collins replied. Little did he know what he was saying.

His best friend, Joe O'Reilly, was with him in Clonmel. Joe did all he could to make the sick man comfortable, but when he tried to tuck Collins in bed the commander in chief snarled at him.

O'Reilly woke at six the next morning. Something told him to leap out of bed and look out of the window. There stood Collins on the steps, a picture of loneliness and dejection as he waited for the armored car that would take him to Cork. O'Reilly, still hurt by Collins' surliness the night before, hesitated a moment, then pulled on his clothes and ran out to say good-by. It was too late; the car had gone. Joe O'Reilly would never cease to regret that he had not got there sooner.

In Cork, one of the Big Fellow's old friends from his prison days came to see him. The friend was for neither one side nor the other in the Civil War. He thought the whole thing was foolish and should be settled as soon as possible to save the nation.

Collins had already promised some of his friends that, once Cork was captured, he might try to reach an agreement with the Republicans. Now Cork was in Government hands.

"Very well," the Big Fellow told his former prison companion. "See me tomorrow night. I may have some news for you."

A gleam like that of the old Collins suddenly lit his eye. "And now," he said to his friend, "what about a bit of ear?" It was his old name for a roughhouse.

"I will not," said his friend. "What would the sentries think if they saw me wrestling with you?"

"They'll do nothing at all," replied Collins. He lunged at his friend, and a moment later they were rolling on the floor in one of the no-holds-barred wrestling matches the Big Fellow loved.

Next morning Collins set out with a party into the mountain country southwest of Cork. They went first to Macroom, to the west, then south to Clonakilty and west to Rosscarbery and Skibbereen. It was late afternoon when they turned north, and near dusk when they struck a back road to Macroom.

Where the narrow road passed through a glen, a few I.R.A. men were waiting in ambush. When the first shots rang out, Collins ordered the cars to halt, and leaped out of the one he was in, his rifle in his hand.

There was a savage fight that lasted an hour. At last the I.R.A. men fled. Collins was not satisfied. He followed them, firing.

Suddenly the others he had left behind became aware that he was no longer firing. Then they thought they heard him call and rushed toward where the sound had come from.

They found Michael Collins there, his head resting on his arms and a big bullet hole in his skull.

The reckless, fearless Big Fellow, with his strange, contradictory character, was gone. He was not only one of the heroes of Ireland's struggle for freedom from 1916 to 1922, but the most colorful of them all. Always the soldier, rising to commander in chief of the Provisional Government army, he had died as he had lived, fighting for what he believed was best for Ireland's future. In the falling darkness his body lay—only a few miles from the place where he had been born, in a beautiful part of Ireland with the blue summits of its mountains rising all around.

Chapter 15

THE HORROR
and the END

THE STORY of how the Civil War went on after Michael Collins' death is incredibly dreadful because of the tactics used by the Irish Free State that succeeded the Provisional Government. One would think that its leaders would have learned a lesson from the British government's execution of the captured leaders in the 1916 Easter Week uprising, but they did not.

The Dáil Éireann assembled in Dublin on September 9 to discuss and vote on the new constitution which would establish a permanent government, as required by the treaty not later than December 6, 1922.

The Republican deputies to the Dáil faced great difficulties. Some were fighting with the Republican army, and others would be arrested if they were caught. And since these thirty-five members were hopelessly outnumbered, anyway, by the fifty-six pro-treaty deputies, it was decided that only one anti-treaty member should attend.

De Valera was persuaded to confer over a possible compromise with General Mulcahy, who had become commander in chief of the Provisional Government army on Michael Collins' death. But the general demanded acceptance of the treaty, and de Valera just as strongly insisted that it was impossible.

William Cosgrave, who had been deputy chairman of the Provisional Government while Collins was its temporary head, was elected president of the Dáil. He appointed his cabinet members and then introduced the bill that included the British-approved treaty, containing the provision for taking an oath of allegiance to the King. It was passed.

On December 6, 1922, the anniversary of the signing of the treaty, the British House of Commons passed a corresponding bill. The Irish Free State was born.

During this session of the Dáil Éireann, the I.R.A. kept on fighting desperately. The strength of the Republican army had been so weakened by the successes of the Provisional Government army that it could no longer make swift raids on enemy posts with small numbers of men, and usually had to use columns of two hundred or more. Yet they did succeed in capturing large quantities of arms and supplies.

Although the Republicans still had the precious *Ballinalee,* its later career was hampered by the increased strength of the Provisional Government army, which now included several armored cars. Nevertheless, it was still a great nuisance to the enemy and General McEóin was determined to capture it.

The *Ballinalee* failed in a raid on Tobercurry, southwest of Sligo, but came back to try again. This time a mine had been rigged on a shelf at its rear. They backed it up to the door of a barracks, but they were unable to drop the mine and blow the place up.

When the *Ballinalee* rolled into Ballina in County Mayo, the place was taken, but the effort was wasted when Free State troops returned and recaptured it. Next, on a road through the Ox Mountains that twisted and turned in sharp curves, the I.R.A. set up an ambush for a Free State force riding in lorries. From concealment, the Republicans opened fire on McEóin's cavalcade.

For a time they had the best of it, but McEóin's men finally fought them off and took ten prisoners. Then an armored car McEóin had obtained joined the fight. Suddenly the *Ballinalee* came thundering out of a side road, and for a time the two monsters dueled. Although the Free State car's driver was shot dead, a relief took his place, and since the *Ballinalee*'s gunner had been killed it was driven off.

McEóin, still determined to capture the *Ballinalee*, sent out three columns of troops with armored cars and an old eighteen-pounder cannon to encircle large numbers of Republicans in northern Leitrim and Sligo counties, and also to get the armored car. He led one column himself. Outside Sligo it reached a bridge the I.R.A. had destroyed. On the other side the *Ballinalee* was waiting, but a well-placed shot from the eighteen-pounder forced it to withdraw.

McEóin's column repaired the bridge and drove the I.R.A. back slowly. His encirclement plan was working well. Although the Republicans fought stubbornly, a hundred were taken prisoner in three days.

The *Ballinalee* was bound to meet its fate now, against other armored cars and the large Free State forces. McEóin learned that the car was proceeding near Benbulben Mountain and set out immediately after it. To his delight, he found that the *Ballinalee* had gone onto a horseshoe-shaped road that doubled back and went nowhere. His men blocked both ends of the road.

The trapped men in the *Ballinalee* dismantled its Vickers

gun and took it with them up the mountain. McEóin's men pursued them, and as the *Ballinalee*'s crew reached the summit, where they could be seen, all five were shot dead. Thus the *Ballinalee*'s gallant career ended.

Fighting, including a naval battle of sorts, continued in counties Sligo and Leitrim. McEóin had one old warship, the *Tartar*. The I.R.A. tried to ambush her in Sligo Bay, but her skipper had made an ironclad out of her with old iron shutters that shielded her from the attackers' bullets while the swivel gun in her bow drove them off.

Although it was winning, the Free State had not stamped out resistance, and gradually it began a military policy much like that used by the British until the 1922 treaty and truce. On September 27, 1923, General Mulcahy asked the Dáil Éireann to allow the army to set up military courts with the power to try any person charged with aiding an attack on the Free State forces, damaging property, possessing unauthorized arms or ammunition or disobeying any army general order or regulation. Punishment might be a fine, imprisonment or death.

There was considerable opposition, but the resolution giving Mulcahy these powers was passed by 47 votes to 15. Before the government began to carry it out, a full pardon was offered to all who turned in arms and ammunition in their possession and ceased to aid the Republicans in any way.

De Valera, who was in Dublin, realized that the Republicans had lost the Civil War, yet he felt they should nevertheless set up an opposition to the new Irish Free State.

This was done, and the opposition was called the Emergency Government. De Valera was unanimously chosen "President of the Republic and Chief Executive of the State." He

selected a Council of State of twelve members, who included
Austin Stack, Robert Barton and Count Plunkett.

Erskine Childers, born in Ireland the son of an English
father and Irish mother, had long been a staunch supporter
of de Valera and full Irish freedom. Both in Ireland and in
England, he had handled important diplomatic work. During the Civil War he had been a staff captain with the Republican army in Munster, but had had no part in the fighting.

In October, 1922, he was summoned to Dublin from hiding
in County Cork to be secretary to de Valera's new Republican government. Childers decided to try and get to Dublin
through the counties of Waterford, Wexford and Wicklow.
He managed to reach the house of his cousin, Robert Barton,
in County Wicklow, only a little south of Dublin, on November 10.

Early the next morning Free State troops surrounded the
house. Childers had an automatic pistol that had been a gift
from Michael Collins. He was ready to use it to fight his way
out of the house, but there were women there and he did not
shoot lest they be harmed, and he was taken.

The next day Winston Churchill, in a speech, said, "I have
seen with satisfaction that the mischief-making murderous
renegade, Erskine Childers, has been captured. No man has
done more harm or shown more genuine malice, or endeavored to bring a greater curse upon the common people of
Ireland than this strange being, actuated by a deadly and
malignant hatred for the land of his birth. . . ." By the last
five words Churchill may have meant England, since Childers' enemies called him an Englishman because of his father's
nationality.

Churchill's words did not help Erskine Childers, in whom
there was not an atom of malice. He was tried on November

17 before an Irish military court for unlawful possession of a pistol. That same day, four Republican prisoners were executed in Dublin on the same charge.

This was the beginning of a period of terror in Ireland so like the executions of Irish prisoners by the British after the 1916 Easter Week rebellion that the world, especially America, was appalled.

Eight other prisoners were tried with Childers on the same charge. They got off with terms of imprisonment, but Childers was sentenced to death. They took him to Beggars Bush Barracks and shot him at dawn on November 24, 1922. Even in England, judges were of the opinion that it was a judicial murder. One deputy to the Dáil resigned in protest.

This was only the beginning. On November 30 three more prisoners were executed for possession of revolvers and bombs. During January, 1923, Republican prisoners were executed in every part of the Irish Free State. Three were shot in Dundalk, County Lough, on January 13, four in Roscrea, Tipperary, and one in Carlow in the county of that name on the 15th. On January 20 eleven more men were executed—two in Limerick, four in Tralee, County Kerry, and five in Athlone, County Westmeath. Hundreds of men who had been captured in the Civil War while armed were in danger of being taken from their prison cells, lined up against a wall and shot.

The Free State army was then given power to impose death for such offenses as possession of documents believed to be against the government's authority, and the army announced that it intended to use this power.

More men were executed. Between November 17 and the end of January, fifty-five prisoners were shot. On February 1, Liam Lynch, a member of the Executive of the I.R.A., announced there would be reprisals if these murders went on.

Meanwhile, the desire for peace had been spreading, not only among the civilian population but also among a number of I.R.A. commandants who believed there was no longer any use in prolonging the Civil War. One of them, General Liam Deasy, issued a statement in which he said: ". . . I will aid an immediate and unconditional surrender of all arms and men, as required by General Mulcahy."

General Deasy asked that de Valera and all the leaders of the Emergency Government do the same. Liam Lynch replied in behalf of these leaders that such a proposal would not be considered.

The almost exhausted Republican army went on fighting as best it could. Its losses became even more severe during that spring of 1923. It was estimated that about 12,000 military prisoners were confined in jails and internment camps. These places were cold, unsanitary and lacking proper medical facilities, and prisoners were often beaten and kicked while being questioned. Some trials were secret, and prisoners under suspended death sentences never knew when their time might come to be marched out and shot. At the end of March, about three hundred women and girls were in prison in Dublin.

Of all the counties of Ireland, beautiful Kerry, with its mountains, lakes and spectacular seacoast, was the most determined not to submit to the Free State government. In one village during March, I.R.A. men set a trap for a Free State officer known to have tortured prisoners. They killed him, two other officers and two civilians.

The Free State retaliated with the worst terror that had yet occurred. Early on the morning of March 7, nine prisoners were marched out of the prison at Tralee. One man had a broken arm, another a broken wrist. At a crossroads, where a log lay with a mine beside it, they were halted. Each man's hands were tied behind him, all were tied together by arms and legs and a rope was put around them so that they formed a circle with their backs to the mine in the center.

The mine was then exploded. Eight men were blown to pieces; one was blown into a ditch only slightly injured and out of sight of the executioners. The Free State officers put the pieces of the eight men into nine coffins, while the lucky prisoner escaped.

The same day in Killarney Prison, five prisoners were taken to a bridge and also blown up by a mine. Again one escaped and lived to report the true story of what had happened. Five more prisoners suffered the same fate at Cahirciveen in Kerry on March 12. In the same month nine more prisoners were executed in several places. In April one I.R.A. man was murdered after surrendering, and his three companions were later executed in Tralee.

During this awful period a prelate of the Catholic Church sent by the Pope himself arrived in Ireland to plead for peace, but the Free State government merely issued a statement saying that its authority could not be interfered with. Then Liam Lynch went from Dublin to visit Republican military leaders in the south and call for a meeting of the Army Executive to try to find a way to end the war honorably without unconditional surrender.

De Valera attended the meeting and submitted proposals he thought might bring honorable peace. But there was disagreement among the officers, some believing that the Republicans should lay down their arms and surrender; others that they should keep on fighting until the Free State showed some willingness to negotiate. The advocates of immediate peace lost in a vote, six to five.

The next few weeks were filled with calamity for the all-but-beaten Republican forces. When the Free State government learned that the Republican leaders were somewhere in the mountain country between Tipperary and Waterford, thousands of troops were sent in to encircle and capture them. On April 10, 1923, while Liam Lynch was in the Knockmealdown Mountains along the Cork-Tipperary border, he and his men discovered an encircling trap of Free State troops. Lynch's party was making its way to freedom when he was shot, and he died in a few hours.

In the same region, on April 14, Austin Stack was captured. A few days later four more commandants of the Republican army were taken. It was rapidly becoming impossible for the I.R.A. to resist any longer.

On April 27, Eamon de Valera, as President of the ill-fated Irish Republic, and Frank Aiken, as chief of staff, issued cease-fire orders to the I.R.A., effective April 30. On that day the Civil War in Ireland came to an end.

The cost in human lives, money and disunity that would haunt Ireland for many years had been staggering. And while the world had approved of Ireland's gallant, hopeless struggle against Britain, the Civil War had brought only shame upon her.

If Ireland had decided to fight rather than accept Britain's treaty terms, she would undoubtedly have been crushed in another bloody struggle, but she would still have had her pride, and in all probability would have risen like the phoenix from the ashes of defeat to gain freedom as so many British possessions have done. Or, if agreement to accept the treaty had been reached earlier, the Irish Free State could have gone on without the shame of the Civil War to gain full freedom in time. The Irish Civil War is a blood-red stain on Ireland's history, as is the American Civil War on America's.

Chapter 16

FREEDOM

EAMON DE VALERA had not for a moment given up the struggle for full Irish freedom when the Civil War ended. He submitted several proposals for the final settlement to Cosgrave, who as President of the Dáil Éireann was head of the Irish Free State. One was that the whole question be submitted to the people of Ireland for a vote. Cosgrave turned down all of de Valera's suggestions.

A general election was set for August 27, 1923. Since several Republican leaders had been arrested by the Free State government, de Valera had gone into hiding. But when a convention of Sinn Fein delegates unanimously called upon him to run for election as a deputy to the Dáil from Clare, he agreed and went there to conduct his campaign. While he was speaking in Ennis, he was arrested by Free State troops.

They kept him under a tight guard and close seclusion in the Arbour Hill Barracks. He was still there, awaiting trial, when the election was held. He received twice as many votes as his rival for the seat in the Dáil.

In October, 1923, he was suddenly transferred to Kilmainham Jail, where he was kept completely isolated from all

174

other prisoners. In the spring of 1924 he was moved back to Arbour Hill. Meanwhile, there was a great clamor for the release of the many political prisoners the Free State was still holding. De Valera's mother went to the United States to obtain support for his release, talked with members of Congress and was the guest of honor at a large gathering held by the American Association for the Recognition of the Irish Republic. On July 16, 1924, de Valera was released.

Not only had he been elected to the Dáil Éireann, but the Republican Party had gained eight seats and now had 44 members against 63 for the Government Party, which gained only five. And in the total vote, the Republicans had about 486,000 votes to 415,000 for the Government Party. However, the Republican deputies could not take their seats in the Dáil because they refused to take the required oath of allegiance to the King.

Dissatisfaction with the settlement the pro-treaty leaders had accepted from Britain was growing in Ireland. Just as Esau, in the Old Testament of the Bible, had sold his birthright to his brother Jacob for a mess of pottage, people began to see that much the same had been done by Ireland. They had believed what Michael Collins had promised: that accepting the treaty would be only the first step toward full freedom. Nothing like that was happening. Britain was still Ireland's lord and master.

Nor were the people happy about the question of Northern Ireland. Under the treaty the six counties of Ulster were to remain a part of Britain. Now there was a serious dispute over the boundary line between Northern Ireland and the Free State.

A Boundary Commission composed of representatives from Britain, Northern Ireland and the Free State was finally organized after a great deal of discussion and dispute. Although the people of southern Ireland wanted a united Ireland, the agreement finally reached by the Boundary Commission was for Partition—the six Ulster counties to remain a part of Britain. It aroused bitter feeling in the Free State that its members of the commission, including Cosgrave, had betrayed them. Partition was to cause continuing trouble for many years to come.

De Valera was now convinced that a new Republican Party should be formed in Ireland. If it could gain enough power, it might be able to take new steps toward full freedom. So in 1926 he organized Fianna Fáil ("Warriors of Destiny").

That Fianna Fáil was already popular with the people of the Irish Free State was proved in the elections of June, 1927. The Government Party's seats in the Dáil Éireann were reduced from 65 to 47. Fianna Fáil elected 44 deputies, while Sinn Fein's members went down from 25 to 5. Fifty-one of the deputies were favorable to the principles of the old Republican Party.

Fianna Fáil could not use its new power in the Dáil Éireann, however, since its members would not take the required oath of allegiance to the King and therefore could not take their seats in the Dáil. A good many of the newly elected Fianna Fáil members had begun to feel that they should sit in the Dáil. One resigned from Fianna Fáil in order to do so; another took the oath and was expelled from the party.

Finally, the party held a meeting and took a vote on the question. It was voted 44 to 7 that the deputies should decide for themselves what to do. Of those who voted for this, 42 felt that the oath was an empty promise and that a deputy who took it could assume that it meant nothing.

Eamon de Valera, always honest and a man who kept his

word when he gave it, was not so sure. He spent agonizing hours wrestling with his conscience. Which was most important—to have Fianna Fáil take an oath to which it was unalterably opposed or to have the new party using its power to win full freedom for Ireland? At last de Valera gave in to the majority—in a way.

The next day he went to Leinster House, where the oath was administered. There he made a statement in Gaelic to the clerk in charge of administering the oath. He said: "I want you to understand that I am not taking any oath or giving any promise of faithfulness to the King of England. . . . I am putting my name here merely as a formality. . . ."

The ceremony was simply a matter of signing a book that contained the oath of allegiance. The clerk said that was all he wanted—the signature. The book was put in front of de Valera. He saw a New Testament lying open and face down on the book.

"Then what is this for?" he demanded. He picked up the Bible, carried it to the other end of the room and laid it down. Then he came back and signed the book, covering what was above the line with some papers.

From then on, de Valera battled relentlessly for his goal of complete independence. In the elections of February, 1932, Fianna Fáil won 72 seats, the largest number of any party in the Dáil. And de Valera was elected President of the Dáil. In May, 1933, he introduced a bill abolishing the oath of allegiance to the King.

However, the constitution still linked Ireland to the King. With great political skill, de Valera took advantage of the abdication of King Edward VIII in 1936 to end this connection.

There was such a furor over the abdication that the British

government ministers had no time to keep an eye on what was going on in Ireland. Just as the abdication was taking place, de Valera's bill removing all reference to the King in the Free State constitution, as well as the British governor-general in Ireland (he had already left anyway), was passed by the Dáil.

However, de Valera wanted to avoid a direct challenge to Britain. So another bill was passed stating that Ireland, as a member of the British Commonwealth of Nations, recognized the King's right to appoint diplomatic and consular officials and make international agreements.

This not only softened the blow but continued the relations with Britain that would be necessary if the two countries were to continue trading with each other—and Britain was Ireland's best customer.

Then, in 1937, a new Irish constitution was approved by both the Dáil and a vote of the Irish people. It declared that Ireland was an "independent and sovereign state" to be called Eire.

Ireland remained neutral during World War II, but the turmoil throughout the world that followed it was much to Ireland's advantage. The vast British Empire began to break up.

Palestine was the first of many regions that had been under British control to gain full independence. The new Zionist state of Israel was proclaimed on May 15, 1948, and Ireland was not far behind.

Eamon de Valera, after heading the Irish government for sixteen years, lost out when Fianna Fáil was defeated in a general election. John A. Costello became Taoiseach, the Gaelic name for Prime Minister. Under his regime, in November, 1948, the Dáil Éireann passed a bill creating the

Republic of Ireland, fully free and no longer a member of the British Commonwealth of Nations.

The new nation was officially proclaimed in a massive celebration of the anniversary of the 1916 uprising, on Easter Monday, 1949. In office or not, de Valera had won the fight that had continued for over thirty years.

Britain's only reaction was insistence that the six counties of Northern Ireland remain a part of Britain, separate from the Irish Republic. Ireland protested strongly, but Partition was kept in effect.

De Valera soon bounced back into office. In the general elections of 1951, Fianna Fáil regained its majority in the Dáil and de Valera was back as Prime Minister.

Ireland also had a President, Séan T. O'Kelly, elected in 1945. In 1959 the two terms allowed him under the constitution ended. Although he was in his late seventies, de Valera was chosen by his party as a candidate for President and was elected.

As this book is written, Eamon de Valera is still President of Ireland. His power in this office is somewhat limited, since the government is largely under the direction of the Taoiseach, or Prime Minister, John Lynch. But although he is eighty-nine years old, his eyesight nearly gone and his health not good, he carries out his duties as President.

He lives in the official presidential mansion in Dublin's Phoenix Park, though he would doubtless prefer to be in his beloved home of Greystones, just outside the city. As President, de Valera takes an active part in the government and receives notable visitors there at Ireland's version of America's White House. He is respected and honored by the Irish people.

No man played a more important part in gaining freedom

for Ireland. De Valera might be compared in that way to the great American patriot Samuel Adams. Sam Adams never gave up his fight to free the American colonies from Britain, even when such patriot leaders as his cousin John Adams, later the second President of the United States, was willing to settle for concessions from Britain rather than a war for independence that seemed hopeless. Eamon de Valera never gave up, either.

As this book is written, one serious flaw in Ireland's independence remains. Partition under the treaty with Britain was the hardest thing for southern Ireland to swallow, and the arrangement has not changed. Unrest in Northern Ireland has continued ever since. In 1971 and 1972 it erupted into violence in which many innocent persons were killed or injured in bomb explosions and sniper fire.

Charges are made that the trouble is solely religious, owing to the persecution of and discrimination against Catholics who live in Northern Ireland by the overwhelming majority of Protestant citizens in the six counties of British-held Ulster or Northern Ireland. It is also charged that the unrest and violence are political.

It would appear that the trouble is due to both causes. There are well-founded charges that the Catholics, who are concentrated chiefly in Belfast and Londonderry (or Derry, as it is more often called), have been discriminated against in favor of Protestants in obtaining employment, and that they have been persecuted in a number of ways.

However, there can be no doubt that southern Ireland, although its government has followed a "hands off" policy in the dispute, would like to see all Ireland united. It would like Ireland's flag to mean what it stands for—the green for southern Ireland, the orange for Northern Ireland. It would like to see persecution of and discrimination against Catholics ended by a united government that would enforce laws against such evils.

On the other hand, the Protestants of Northern Ireland are fiercely determined to remain a part of Britain. Their chief leader, the head of the Church of England in Ulster, is a vociferous and unyielding man on this subject.

And so, in 1972, the violence continues. The I.R.A., outlawed in the Irish Republic, remains organized in Ulster, and much evidence points to its guilt in most of the violence. To combat it, Britain has been forced to send in large numbers of troops to keep order and try to stop the bombings. And despite its efforts to avoid the mistakes of 1916-22, there have been countercharges of violence against the Catholics by these British soldiers.

Where will it end? No one knows now, in early 1972. In many ways the problem seems more difficult to solve than that of the long struggle to establish the free and independent Republic of Ireland. Yet that was finally solved. It is to be hoped that the one of Northern Ireland will also be, and in a much shorter time.

SUGGESTED FURTHER READINGS

By far the best, most accurate and extensively researched book on the Irish Republic from its beginnings in 1916 is Dorothy MacArdle's *The Irish Republic*. It not only contains the full story in over 800 (paperback edition) pages, but also has reproductions of many important statements and documents, thumbnail sketches of the Irish leaders executed in 1916, a bibliography of 150 or more reference sources and an excellent index. Any student of Irish history, especially the struggle that won freedom for Ireland, will do well to consult this book.

Eamon de Valera, by the Earl of Longford and Thomas P. O'Neill, on which President de Valera himself cooperated with the authors in their work, is certainly an outstanding story of the life of one of Ireland's great men.

Nora Connolly O'Brien, daughter of James Connolly, has told an important and most interesting story of her memories, her father and the part she played in the Easter Week rising of 1916 in *The Unbroken Tradition*. Under her maiden name, she also wrote the biographical *Portrait of a Rebel Father*. Both are well worth reading.

Frank O'Connor's *The Big Fellow* is the story of Michael Collins—an interesting and exciting biography.

Of the many other sources, *Peace by Ordeal,* by Frank Pakenham (later the Earl of Longford), is a highly respected and scholarly account, especially for its details regarding the long series of negotiations with England which took place. Max Caulfield's *The Easter Rebellion* is another excellent book on Easter Week of 1916, and *Ireland's Civil War,* by Calton Younger, is a very complete story of that part of Ireland's struggle for freedom.

BIBLIOGRAPHY

Caulfield, Max. *The Easter Rebellion.* New York: Holt, Rinehart & Winston, 1963.

Connolly, Nora (see also O'Brien, Nora Connolly). *The Unbroken Tradition.* New York: Boni & Liveright, 1918.

Fox, R. M. *Green Banners.* London: Secker & Warburg, 1938.

Harrison, G. B. (editor). *The Letters of Queen Elizabeth.* New York: Funk & Wagnalls, 1968.

Kerryman, Ltd. *Dublin's Fighting Story, 1913-1921, told by the men who made it.* Tralee: The Kerryman, Ltd., no date.

Longford, the Earl of, and O'Neill, Thomas P. *Eamon de Valera.* Boston: Houghton Mifflin, 1971.

MacArdle, Dorothy. *The Irish Republic.* London: Transworld Publishers, 1968.

MacLochlainn, Piaras F. *Last Words.* Dublin: Kilmainham Jail Restoration Society, 1971.

MacManus, Seumas. *The Story of the Irish Race.* New York: Devin, Adair, 1970.

McCarthy, Joe. *Ireland.* New York: Time, Inc., 1964.

McHugh, Roger. *Dublin, 1916.* London: Arlington Books, 1966.

Moody, T. W., and Martin, F. X. (editors). *The Course of Irish History.* New York: Weybright & Talley, 1967.

O'Brien, Nora Connolly. *Portrait of a Rebel Father*. Dublin: Talbot Press, 1935.

O'Brien, R. Barry (editor). *Two Centuries of Irish History, 1691-1870*. London: Trench, Trubner, 1907.

O'Connor, Frank. *The Big Fellow*. London: Corgi Books, 1969.

Pakenham, Frank (see also Longford, the Earl of). *Peace by Ordeal*. London: Jonathan Cape, 1935.

Rowse, A. L. *The Expansion of Elizabethan England*. New York: Harper & Row, 1965.

Schuneman, Peter. *Ireland*. New York: Hill & Wang, 1961.

Smith, Goldwyn. *A History of England*. New York: Scribner, 1966.

Spindler, Karl. *Gun Running for Casement in the Easter Rebellion, 1916*. London: W. Collins Sons, 1921.

———— *The Mystery of the Casement Ship*. Berlin: Kribe-Verlag, 1931.

Ward, Lock & Co., Ltd. *A Pictorial and Descriptive Guide to Dublin and Its Environs*. London: Ward, Lock, 1923.

Younger, Calton. *Ireland's Civil War*. New York: Taplinger, 1969.

INDEX

ABOUT THE AUTHOR

Clifford Lindsey Alderman was born in Springfield, Massachusetts and graduated from the United States Naval Academy at Annapolis. Much of his subsequent career was as an editor and in public relations work in the field of shipping and foreign trade, but during World War II he returned to naval service.

Mr. Alderman has written historical novels for adults and both fiction and non-fiction for young people. He believes in knowing firsthand the places of which he writes and has traveled extensively in Europe, Canada, the West Indies and throughout the United States.

He lives with his wife in Seaford, New York.